NIGHT WORK
THE SAWCHUK POEMS

NIGHT WORK
THE SAWCHUK POEMS

Randall Maggs

The question that he frames in all but words
Is what to make of a diminished thing.

– Robert Frost, "The Oven Bird"

Brick Books

Library and Archives Canada Cataloguing in Publication

Maggs, Randall
     Night work : the Sawchuk poems / Randall Maggs.

ISBN 978-1-894078-62-7

1. Sawchuk, Terry—Poetry. 2. Hockey—Poetry. 3. Hockey
goalkeepers—Biography—Poetry. I. Title.

PS8576.A348N53 2008   C811'.54   C2007-905652-0

We acknowledge the Canada Council for the Arts, the Government of
Canada through the Book Publishing Industry Development Program
(BPIDP), and the Ontario Arts Council for their support of our
publishing program.

Cover image: *The Toronto Star*.

Author photograph by Anne LeMessurier.

The book is set in ITC Galliard and Helvetica.

Design and layout by Alan Siu.

Printed and bound by Sunville Printco Inc.

Brick Books
431 Boler Road, Box 20081
London, Ontario N6K 4G6

www.brickbooks.ca

This book is for my brother, Darryl, who saw it all for himself. And for our mother, who wouldn't look up from her lap whenever he was on the ice.

There are multiple fine scars present over the
forehead and the face. The most prominent lies
in the midfrontal region and is an oblique
scar, 1 ½" in length, which extends from the
midline below and to the right, ending at the
upper margin of the right eyebrow. Suture
cross scars are present, of a fine character,
along the course of this healed scar. There is
an old, oblique, linear scar, 3/4", extending
across the midthird of the left eyebrow. There
is present, at the anterior aspect of the
hairline on the left side, approximately 2 ½"
above the left eyebrow, an old, faint, linear
scar, 3/4 by ¼", that lies 1 ½" to the left of
the midline. There is a flattening of the
prominence at the junction of the bony portion
of the nasal bone and the cartilaginous septum.
There is an old, vertical, linear scar present
over the right side of the upper lip, 3/8"
medial to the angle of the mouth. It measures
3/8" vertical. Extending across the upper lip
from the left nostril is an old irregular scar,
7/8 by 1/8", that ends at the mucocutaneous
border ¼" to the right of the midline. An old,
fine, linear scar, 3/8" by 1/8", extends from
the mucocutaneous border of the lower lip on
the right side, at a point 3/4" to the right of
the midline. There are three, fine, old,
linear scars present in the midline,
transversely beneath the lower lip, the largest
of which measures ¼".

(from the autopsy of TERRANCE GORDON SAWCHUK, Case No.
4468, PERFORMED BY DR. GROSS, ASSOCIATE MEDICAL
EXAMINER: In the presence of Drs. Helpern, Beaghler, and Hyland,
and Dr. Richard Tiedemann, Surgical Resident of New York Hospital:
May 31,1970.)

Contents

III. TWO GOALIES GOING FISHING IN THE DARK

VIII. LAST MINUTE OF PLAY

I. THE QUESTION THAT HE FRAMES

The way sorrow enters the bone
is with stabs and hoverings.

> – Denise Levertov,
>   "The Blue Rim of Memory"

Neither Rhyme nor Reason

In the old films, the ice looks more like winter,
the boards were boards and clear. I see the lone official
out for a skate, flipping a puck in the air. He seems
in no rush for the teams to appear, his long stride
preoccupied and familiar. He swings by again
and I see it's him, Red Storey, younger here
than that long afternoon in his home
with his souvenirs and second wife.
        I think of him there in his chair, his legs
wrapped in a blanket. He lifts his hands and looks at them
absently, turning them slowly back to front, the massive hands
that sent off Harvey and Howe, placated the Rocket and Lindsay
and Eddie Shore. He says she taught him how to use a spoon
again and hold a pen and clear the clutter of his memory.
Now she's taking his old brick house apart, peeling
the years from his walls, pulling down shadowy
paper, looking for the house beneath.

What were you thinking of, Red, gliding by
so long ago? How ragged the ice in the Forum seemed
after Detroit? How to keep the crowd from lynching bloody Lindsay?
Or that subtler trouble with Sawchuk, who'd lead the Red Wings
onto the ice? He'd told his first wife about that moment,
the two teams slowly circling, tension building, and Terry
veering over to ask that crazy question.

Where to begin with the guy? Even after 50 years,
it nags him like a wrinkle on his ankle. *What he came to me
wanting to know, Jesus, I thought he was joking.*

The winter day gives in. He tugs the blanket close
around his knees, but even as I rise in the darkening room
to go, the voice begins again. The talk on trains. Lindsay waiting
in the tunnel and waving a stick in his face. A voice in Boston
that could rub the skin right off you. *Hey, Storey, ya bum!
We got a town down here named after you!*

Finally his wife appears to mention the hour,
reaching in to switch on the light. You hear an edge
to her voice too, a toughness you'd want in any scrap
with time. Out in the hallway, the acid fumes
of wallpaper stripper, her warning
to watch the icy steps.

The First Wife

In old films the ice looks grey,
you half expect a trampling of cows at the edge,
an arc of grain the cutter missed as it turned.

The camera seems left on accidentally,
awaiting the teams coming onto the ice. A chair scrapes.
"Are we on yet?" someone asks, the voice unhurried, unrattled
by any heresy of unused air. The crowd arriving in hats
and ties. The gleam of newly flooded ice. The graceful stride
of the only man on the ice. As large as Storey is, there's ice enough
and time to think before he turns to drop the puck
and start the game.

               Snow in the street lights after,
heading home. The beckoning lights of familiar bars.
God how he loves this city. Idling at a red on Sherbrooke Street,
his mind swings back to that puzzling talk with Terry,
then his turning abruptly away towards his goal.
One set of lights, and he'd be home on Beaconsfield
with his wife and the kettle on in the kitchen.
And why would you fret about Sawchuk
anyway? Jumping Jesus, what the guy could do.
He'd felt the agony in the Forum tonight, the agitated
crowd, and Irvin back and forth like a dog behind the Montreal
bench, throwing up his hands, bending in anger to one of his players
as Terry turned them back wave after wave in the terrible storm
of the crowd—48 shots against 12, the Rocket in twice,
but the Wings take the game 3 to 1.

And Storey, as he did so often when he drove,
talking away in his head with his wife.
Would he mention it once he was home, he wondered,
with a mug of tea to warm his hands? Maybe yes, maybe no.
There wasn't much rhyme nor reason to what you did or didn't
say to wives. And when you had your well-handled game,
much order or sense to anything else.

II. KINGS AND LITTLE ONES

You said, "I will go to another land,
I will go to another sea."

– C. P. Cavafy, "The City"

Initia Gentis

All my life I'll know this restless tilt of eyes,
the upward glance before you get set, how much
time to save your skin.

Begins in school the trouble
with time. Winter's bright brief days, but afternoons
that never seem to end. The black hand's gloom.

No lights on the North End rinks, they let us
get into our gear at lunch for the game after school.
We pretend not to notice—what's the big deal, sharpen
a pencil in shoulder pads, sing for your music mark
in your jock. The nervous scratch of pens as we wait our turn
for the music test. Kshuba glances up again, *come on, come on*
you clock, and sags when he hears Miss Nelson call his name,
though she was never one to joke about our names.
And this was a day she wore the famous blouse.

Dip the nib and scrawl of hoops while we wait,
diminishing O's, tortured over what to sing and where,
standing by your desk or up at hers, she gave you that. Kshuba's
crumpling number as he bends toward her ear. The pens stop.
"Listen," Eileen Chalkman whispers. "It's God Save the Queen."
Miss Nelson glances at the class, the giggling stopped cold
by the look in her eyes, winter butterflies.
Hardly more than a murmur, his painful groping
for the tune, his voice rising, descending to a moan.
Kshuba, who never hears a word of English in his home,
whose one big fear is looking like a fool.

"Send her victorious hoppy and glorious."

A suicidal wheezing in the room.
Stifled hysteria. Loyal team-mates too.

On the ice you pay the price. And he went after everyone
that afternoon, hogged the puck, pounded Gordie Biggar
up against the boards, and bit the referee. "Okay Okay," he says,
walking home, "I should sing for her *Farmer by a Rock?
Sergeant Hooper's Troopers?*"

We cut across the vacant lot,
heading for the cooking smells we knew,
the woodsmoke hanging over clapboard houses
in the cold, twelve years old and troubled by our difficult names
and dreams (the blouse that made your hair stand up).
Shuffling along in his gear and galoshes, he starts
singing *Sergeant Hooper's Troopers.* We sing it together,
not the brassy mocking way we belt it out in the dressing room,
unnerving the other team, but slow and sad like lonely riders
with their cattle in the rain, or cousins on barren farms
in the old country, imagining our green
and perfect garden.

Sheet Metal

MacDonald's Sheet Metal in East Kildonan,
where Louis his father found work. Weekends, he'd take
Terry on a job, once to build hoods for a new bakery's ovens.
Late one night that winter—he'd stayed to help flood
the rinks—he hurries by the bakery in the dark.
He smells the fresh-baked bread and rolls and glimpses
shadows bending at the open oven doors. He shakes his frozen
fingers in the cold. He knows his mother won't be happy
when she hears he's lost his gloves. Man, to buy a nickel bun
still steaming from those ovens, to feel its heat
a moment in your hands.

Louis was born in Austria, a Ukrainian. A strong
but gentle man, shaped by the sound of violins
and un-flat land. One fight in his life, his uncles told Terry,
one punch, and he knocked his man cold, a boxer too. Another time
in the shop, they said, on a seemingly endless Friday afternoon,
Louis went mental, shouting, shaking a big sheet of metal
over his head, making it wobble and thunder—*Prokofiev!*
Here comes the wolf! Here comes the tympani!!
Then quietly laid it back down on his bench
to mark off Monday's ducts and flashing.

A walking accident, it seemed, like many
displaced men. A connoisseur of cuts and wounds,
he'd turn a wrist to show his son the latest gash.
One winter playing in Galt, Terry was told his father
had broken his back. He was with the Wilson brothers
when he heard, hanging out in front of the post office,
mocking snooty Ontario girls. Walked right off the scaffolding,
they said. Must have been a Friday afternoon.

Cutting patterns in the cold, Terry wore gloves
like his father, thin so you could make a proper curve.
But he was wary of corners and edges and met with an accident
only once, slipping on ice on a dazzling Winnipeg winter day,

slicing open his catching hand. They taped it back
together and carted him off to the clinic. "So, Louis,"
his uncle Nick muses, half to ease a nephew's
fear, "I wonder who's his father's son?"

Years later, Pulford would skate across
that same hand as Terry slid out to smother a shot.
The way his fingers hung loosely down, the tendons severed,
he thought they were gone. "Don't take your glove off yet, kid,"
Kelly said. Before they got over to Lefty and the bench,
he remembered his uncle's joke and the leap
of white light like a sword in the sun.

The Dog Behind the Stove

Terry's sister lies there wide awake.
She hears the clunk of logs below, then the sinking
confirmation of a slamming pan. The stove lid rattles in fury
at her father's placating murmur. A top stair creaks—
Terry, wanting to be out and gone to the rink.

She senses an altered light at her window, a sign
of spring. The outer kitchen door would be open to cool
things off. Judy is thinking the birds will soon be back.
If she could fly. If she could fly like them and join
their shrill and lifting songs, ribboning out a satin gown
of her own. Her mother's voice begins to rise again.
Then under her window the mailman coming up the step,
a scrabble of claws on the kitchen floor and a crash
as the dog goes after him through the screen.

Letters everywhere. Helping to pick them up,
she feels the softening crust beneath her slippered feet.

Later she sits at the kitchen table, watching her father
squaring a pile of crumbs, one of his faraway
games. The winter door is closed again and the screen door
dangles on a shattered frame. Judy thinks about a large and broken
bird, a solitary awkward crane, whose only hope was immobility
and keeping silent as a stick. "Have to get at that pretty quick,"
she hears her father say, "before the mosquitoes
hatch and eat us alive."

The dog lifts his head suspiciously. She sees
he's back where he likes to lie, behind her mother's stove,
an adopted Alsatian devoted to her who, through it all,
hadn't said a word, hadn't even turned when Terry left, dragging
his pads half through, half past the broken door. Judy watches
the shoulder moving with the wooden spoon. She hears
the handle rap against the rim, and deep in the pot,
the jubilant boiling all over again.

The Back Door Open Where She's Gone to the Garden

A nervous quiet in the house, no hello
to get a bearing from. My sister at the kitchen table,
staring out the open door. "She's gone to the garden,"
she says. "She wants to make kasha for supper
tonight." I hear an adult sadness in her voice.
"You had another argument I guess."

The stove is out, the kitchen so quiet I hear
the drying spices near the door. Outside, the day feels
tropical for September. Still, such a departure—
it's not like her to leave any door open.

There's something like a question in the air.
Now that she's lost a second son, she hardly speaks,
and I'm too quick to take offence, thinking she'd rather
it was me. Now I'm helpless here. Try to bridge
the widening gap—she'd only think it weak of me.
How do the rest of us deal with him being gone?
My sister up in her room with her illnesses, looking out
her window at the street. And I wear the pads in the family
now. I bring the bruises home, the aches and taunts
that wake me in our moon-bleak room.

She's gone to my father's garden,
something else she rarely does, until she has him
flood it for a rink. It's his still and private shelter more than ever
now. I've watched him disappear between the rows, pulling weeds
and winding tendrils onto strings. The days grow shorter
as he tilts his head and sniffs the air for frost.
Right to the last, he'll tend the cantaloupe and grapes
that haven't a hope of ripening here. He'll choose a green tomato
for his eggs. Or stop to see what's happening at the cucumber frame.
A background man. He'll stand for such a long long time,
I'll lose him in the vines until he moves.

The Famous Crouch

A fierce moon at the window hunting boys.
An attic room my brother shared with me, the good warmth
diving under quilts on winter nights, four steps
from the bucket to the bed.

And laughing in the dark at how old goalies
held their sticks, all knuckled up, and how they combed their hair.
I'd tell Mitch that he was mental playing goal,

but always help to scrape the ice before he played.
Then stamp a flat spot on the bank behind him, changing ends
when he changed ends. "Terry, keep your fingers off the screen,"
he'd warn me, once he'd kicked the puck away.

He clasped his hands behind his head (they said),
behind his desk at work that day and stretched and yawned,
content (he'd shut out St Vitale the night before and he'd seen
Corinne Wynick in the crowd), and smiling, cocked
his head to make a final point (they said),
half rose, and then pitched forward on his face.

All those nights I'd hear him
in his sleep. *Stay low, stay forward, balance
on a ball. Forget the names they sing you through the screen.
See the shot before it leaves the stick.*

Such preparedness, I'd lie awake and think.

And so I got accustomed to the view from here.
You watch them come at you in waves
and watch them fly away. In my dreams he plunges
after the puck, then turns to find me grabbing at the screen.
But now it's me who's bending low and looking for
the bullet shot. All my life, I'd heard the warning
in his voice and in the moment's heat
I hear it yet.

Writing on the Walls

Ever rode the train before? I heard the lazy
voice and saw the sleepy eyes appraising what I'd worn
into the world. A red hockey jacket. A pair of my brother's pants.
I felt for the ten dollar bill in a pocket, still folded, my mother
had pressed it into my hand on the porch. Too quick,
I answered sure I had. He grinned and slid across
to make some room. "Art Arthurs is the name,"
he said, "Kings and Little Ones is the game,"
his voice a drawl, introducing the others,
all forgotten long ago,
while I see him on every train.

Travelling east, the stubble fields gave way
to endless trees. Bored, I'd shouldered past the blast
between the cars, the air that reeked of piss and creosote,
the odour of the world it seemed to me.
I liked the bar car too, the smoke that curled
from ashtrays into the lights, the hushed and knowing
laughter at the tables. Unfolded, the bill brought me
into the game and luck at first, and the certainty her fears
were only a mother's fears, with a careful margin
of error. Art Arthurs watched the growing pile
in front of me and winked at the crest
on my sleeve—"Lookit there boys,
old number one. I guess we should of seen
the writin' on the walls."

Outside, the day flashed past unseen,
the fences down in bogs, the piles of stone,
the level crossings clanging in the dark. The game sped on.
The northern lights, like Cossacks, leapt at stars. Such dancers,
my mother said her mother would say, brilliant dancers,
like all barbarians, but beasts with women and fire.
I wanted to know these things for myself.
After the game, Art Arthurs led us
back to the dining car. I wanted into his country

where trainmen knew to pull aside for speeding freights,
where people took passing acquaintance in stride, winning
and losing, the puffed-up waiters in the dining car.

"First time," he'd said, leaning back and looking up
at ours, "first time I ever had a square meal
off a round plate."

I would have sent home what she gave me, doubled,
just so she'd know, but I didn't know how
to get out ahead of the game.

I might have learned that then about myself.

"Say, what about livin' dangerously,"
Art Arthurs had said. "One last hand before I take us
to dinner and winner takes all?"

I sat awake until morning and there they were
again, the trees and fallen fences rushing by. All night,
I'd heard his gentle mocking voice.
Ever rode the train before?
As if there was only one, and a hell of a thing
to get off.

Hole in the Hat

(i)

28 December, 1947. *Lucky boy*, they said,
you missed the war. Half a season in Omaha, his first
as a pro. A patched-up eye, a cumbersome collar to hold his head
steady, felt like he was on the troop train home.

A month before, the team
on the bus travelling south, jogged awake, he sees a red sun
rising over bitten land. Snake rocks. Cactus. An hour from Houston,
the radiator blows. Sickly green all over the road. Local travellers
slow their trucks, squint across their sunburnt arms,
asking what in hale we disembowelled.

Texas. Jesus. Boulevards with palms. Trees
with bean pods two feet long. Foolish place to play
hockey in the first place. Plants and bugs
with teeth. Mexican tiles.

(ii)

An oval of faces floating overhead,
green masks and goggles. Four eyes. Frog eyes.
This is where they'd gone, the brainy guys. And here's
a mindlessness he's grown to love, morphine wings, hearing the talk
on the bus again, Geisebrecht and Simon hatching plans—Agar,
son of a bitch, the rip he'd given Geisebrecht a week before,
and worse, the grin when he walked around them both
to win the game. "Give him a look up the middle,"
says Geisebrecht. "Lure the son of a bitch with an open lane."

Converging in front, they catch him high and low,
high stick, cross-check, arse-over-kettle into the crease.
A skate arcs lazily past, the stick accelerates in anger
or science, cracks Terry in the eye.

He hits the ice like a pallet of stone.

(iii)

The ice feels cool against his face, relief
at last, this godforsaken place. Then the voices
wake him and he frowns. And what's this weight
like an egg on his cheek and why can't he
see? And what had he heard them say
before he woke? Saving one and *let the other go?*
But hell, you have to laugh, that monster eye behind
the lens. And knowing you must be just a thing
when someone looks that close. He knows
this all too well, the breath on his face, the loop
of thread and tug at his flesh. The masks lean close
for one last look, then, mercifully, the light goes out.

(iv)

Darkest night of his life, once the morphine
seeped away. He wept and prayed. A one-eyed
goalie, not much use to anyone. But fell asleep at last
and woke to a promising haze, and promptly
forgot all his bargains, hastily made.

His first game at home, he shuts down St. Paul
in a bitter, familiar wind. *The hole in the hat*, they said.
The bent badge. He wouldn't be the first or last to dodge
one here in Texas. Lucky, he missed the wars,
and down he goes and who just happened
to be in Houston with his plane delayed?—
Sir This or That, some brilliant eye surgeon
from Britain, tops in his field. Still, he had a time
of it, they said, had to pop the eyeball out to stitch it up.
Couple of days, it was touch and go. But, healed and back
on the ice, who's good as new? Who's better?—
23 of 27 games he wins, Rookie of the Year,
and look who's on the road again.

Just a little bump along the way.

Stations of the Cross

Santa Maria ora pro nobis.
— from *The Litany of the Saints*

(i) *Annie the mother*

Perched on the edge of Terry's bed, half-turned,
like the lady up on the needle-nosed horse on the wall
in the nurse's room. Riding crop in her fine-boned hand.
A groom attending keeps a wary eye on the hand.
Unlikely pose for his mother, more hers the solid stance,
slapping dough or clanking shut the stove lid.

Or square above the boards against the sky, wearing
her husband's galoshes. Her fierce gaze follows
the ankled-over hiving on the rink below.

The room that Terry shares with his older brother.
And over Mitch's bed, a grinning Turk Broda jokes trouble
away, and Frankie Brimsek coolly measures the camera.
Mr Zero. The shutout king. Moonlight shifts across
the bedroom walls, asking Terry where
his brother is tonight.

Across the room a badly made bed.
That morning, Mitch was up and out to shovel
the backyard rink before he went to work.

His goal pads dragged across the room's dividing line.
The sausage folds, straps that Mitch would
angle out a leg to fasten tight.
Leather's reassurance.

Her hand smooths Terry's unmarked brow.
Not for her the expectation of a country life, of riding
side-saddle into the drizzling woods,
sherry after, a crackling fire.

(ii) *the nurse from northern Mexico*

A ceiling fan ticks over, shifting
weighted air. White blouse leaning over
close and white, the desert moon. Her eyes and face
as dark as mine. Your pads are put away, she says and smiles.
A practised hand slides up my leg, removing the last
of my gear. I glimpse the mischief in her eyes.
Heartless, mothers, *always clean socks, you never know when,*
but what have we here? Lawdy. Short pants
and a garter belt. In Texas too.

That night I dreamt about the rink
behind our house, my friends gone home,
and my father dragging a hose along the bank to flood the ice.
She woke me through the night to cool me off, a cloth on my face
like ice in the crease when you first go down.

(iii) *the woman and the famous wind*

And one who seldom slept our few short nights
together over the years. I see the dates blocked out
on her calendar—*Wings in Town.* Older part of Chicago,
hunching brick in the wind. Put off the bed, the cat sits
a moment drowsy, dishevelled, then starts to wash
himself. Pretends it's all one to him.

Her fingers brush over my face. She knows
my history, travelling from scar to scar. Brow to cheek
to chin. Naming names.

Her soft insistent voice, the tone you take
with a nervous animal. I sense her shifting over me
in the dark, her leg lifting carefully over my face.

A marvellous hinge a woman's hip.

Her whisper grows harsher, blends with traffic
in the rain.

Night Shift

The floating faces after surgery—angels
or nurses, I don't care. Wherever I've been seems
better to me, but, waking, I hide the crankiness
I feel. Someone lifts my arm to help me turn
and snugs the flimsy gown along my legs.
Then the visitors with rumours and bouquets,
too assured of their place in the world, it seems to me.
Somewhere out of sight, they ask for jars. Mother of God,
the agony of abdominal gas—what do I want
with gossip and flowers?

And doubled up all night, my Christ,
what a life. Like Pompeii's dead, my arse in the air,
bare. I don't care.

The light from the hall washes over the wall
toward my bed where the hospital gown rides up my back.
I hear the soft laughter from the door. She's different
in everyday clothes, distinctly amateur, reaching beneath me
to tie my gown and tug the wrinkles from the sheet. When she leans
closer, I catch a hint of the bar where she's left her friends.
Also an odour of earth and leaves.

Who starts the brain's conspiracies?
Who knows what it is that waits in the trees?
Crazy. To leave your friends and risk the park at night.
To pass the stolen flowers through the bars, lift her skirt
and reach a leg up over the deadly staves.

She knows the cupboard where they keep
the jars. I wake in the odour of daffodils, with the beat
of an old school poem in my head, and a half-dread
so familiar in these dangerous days.

A Clever Dog

If you can find anyone who's got anything good
to say about Jack Adams, tell him to give me a call.
                          – Glenn Hall, on the phone

(i)

After the game, the last of the press gone,
won over to his way of seeing again—*Jack oh Jack,*
they said, *you are a clever dog*—yet another brilliant thought
emerged. The time was right. Bring Sawchuk down
to Windsor for a week, that should do the trick.
Let him look across the river at the lights.

You'd hardly say he set the town on fire. He only
got into half a dozen games, and what with all that skyline
seemed to offer, not to mention the French Canadian girls
who hung around the rink (brazen the way they looked
right back at your look), his play was little more
than mediocre. *So what's the fuss*, said one of the Spitfires
lifting a puffy brow, though some had learned to know
the glow that marks the chosen few.

And Jack was Jack, and well aware of what
Terry could do. So why give a horse's fart what happened
on the southern side? And south of the river, that's where Terry
was in that moment, looking across at the lights, though
he'd have said Windsor was north of Detroit.
Tricky geography here, easy to get turned around.
What the skyline blotted out was Canada.

Tomorrow, he'd take the train across
to Detroit. Laboured cough, lurch and clank,
trains were the noise of the world to him. Up on the trestle,
something rat-shaped rippled over the ties, inking out
lights as it went. While Jack across the river
signed a check and closed his door.

(ii)

Late as it was, something drew him all the way
to the top. He stopped abruptly where the vastness
opened out, where a sudden gaping took his breath away,
and far below and ghostly in the maintenance lights,
the fabled Olympia ice. His ice.
Nothing to equal it anywhere in the world.
Why was he wanting space tonight? Something
looming, he supposed. He looked across at the clock
with its Export sign and its smiling Highland girl. He liked
the view from up here, although he found something unsettling
about that woman, larger than life, and all those empty seats.
He never liked the sight of empty seats. He glanced
at the ice again, miles away it seemed with its whispery
sheen, its mirrored nets, a nagging absence in each crease.
One thing he knew without a shade of doubt, wherever
the weary goalies were in that moment, whatever comfort
the night had brought their aching limbs, their minds
were here, making the crucial plays all over again.
This was what Jack knew better than anyone else—
whatever happened of importance in the building happened
in between those blood-red posts. He thought of Durnan's courage
tonight, his wild abandon diving into the pile. Something *lifted*
inside him (that was the word). He thought of the best
he'd battled himself, Vezina, maybe, or Benedict
with his leather mask, or Gardiner, the fierce little Scot,
the first to charge out of his crease to challenge the shooters.
A great going out was what he felt himself, and love
(again that was the word), but this was followed
by a dizziness and on its heels a fright.
He reached out a hand for the rail.
He'd had enough of open space, of standing
eye to eye with the clock, never mind that cool
assessing gaze—whatever she had on her mind or under
that kilt was of limited interest to him. He wondered about it

sometimes—why couldn't his players leave the women
alone? Fractious encounters were more to his taste.
He'd been a savage himself in front of the net.
Now what he needed, he knew, was something
to clamp in his teeth, a good cigar, the clutter and funk
of his office and someone to straighten out. He did
have that meeting with Sawchuk coming up—
three thousand? What the devil was he
thinking? He'd tear up the check and make out
another for two. He sensed his team was on the verge
of doing some damage and Terry had all the skills to change
the game, but if he couldn't take the heat or got himself
hurt, he'd be out of here as fast as last year's hat.
Who did Jack already have but Harry Lumley,
no slouch in anyone's eyes, and then that other kid
they'd signed on a whim, what's-his-name Hall—
he'd have to dump the pond-hockey stance,
but he was quick and called you sir.
Another pussycat, you'd have to think.

He settled himself in his chair to wait
for Terry's knock at the door. *I am a clever dog,*
he thought, *and in the pink.*

The Question for Harry

You hardly thought of Harry Lumley as a little guy,
but Terry was having trouble getting his sweater
over his head. Who'd think a guy so big could move that quick.
In practice, the players had poked and prodded with their seeming
casual shots, sniffing out a spot where he was soft. Wherever
they put one, he was waiting. Circling back, preoccupied,
they'd test the flex of their sticks on the ice. The kid
was a comer. The only question for Harry,
they figured, was when.

The guys getting dressed beside him wouldn't help,
so Harry knew it was up to him, cursing his crutch and himself
for a fool. What was he thinking, grabbing the puck and piling up
the ice? It just made him crazy, sometimes, the way the others
could wind it up behind his net, or whirl and take off
out of their end, slapping their sticks for a pass.

One-handed, he gripped the sweater near the number,
his number, hauling it down, something welling, as always,
helping a team-mate into his armour. Big as Harry was, though,
how would he really feel if the kid fell flat? Friend or foe,
for goalies it got fuzzy here. He felt the shallow
breathing under his hand. "You get that first shot, Kid,
you'll be okay." He tugged out the wrinkles
and flattened the number.

Said Harry, the team's old man at 23, having
his best year yet, before he started clowning and tore up
his knee. The dressing room was quiet. They knew the name
of the game—who bought a house in Detroit with Adams
running the show? Still, a team-mate after all, a decent guy,
you felt like hell. While Jack was having a tough time hiding
his grin, watching his two big goalies together, watching the kid
struggle up for air, knowing Harry was headed the other way.
The fit was tight, but it wasn't as if you had much choice.
There was only one sweater with 1 on the back,
and the message abundantly clear.

Jitters

A goalie likes to get that first shot early in the game.
– Jacques Plante

Up and up and up the brilliant ascension
into Olympia. Saving Harry Lumley,
it seemed a happy convergence of dreams,
the gallery gods were out in force and noisy that night.
When he missed that first shot, a floater, the shock
was like your ladder pulled away.
"Don't trade Lumley yet," someone got off
a good one up in the greys. A mediocre shot, the puck
seemed to pass right through his hand. A conspiracy of matter.
Jitters was all he offered the press, neglecting to mention
the friendly fire, three of the four goals in off his own
defence, forgot the loss, but not the foghorn voice,
no, all night fucking long that voice,
and he played the shot a thousand times
on his bedroom ceiling where the street light shone.

Nonetheless, the team was into its golden age
with Terry, as Adams predicted. Three years out his five
in Detroit he walked away with the Vezina, though
the one he thought about most was one he lost
by a single goal, a bouncing shot
the last game of the year.
"What a way to lose a thousand bucks."
He groped in his shirt for a match. "Bloody
bouncing shots." He blew out the smoke and downed
his drink. That summer they made him insane,
he'd sweat through the night and jerk
wide awake, pucks bouncing
every which way in his darkened room.

But on his game he was trouble. Sometimes
you hardly saw the point of showing up. 1952, Year
of the Octopus, he sweeps both Toronto and Montreal.
Five goals he gives up in eight games. And shuts them

down in all four games at home. The seats clap back.
The hats come tumbling down. The gods lean out
below the smoky beams and cheer the circling
goalie hoisted high. The party that night
goes on and on as if it could never end. Glasses
raised. Grips of camaraderie. The goaltender
at the heart of it all. The couples move
out of the clubhouse to dance on
the greens. Dizzy, they tumble
into the bunkers unseen and
laughing lie there and drink
to the moon. Spring, and wild
in the air, the lilac scent of love
and dynasty. Oh immortality. The city
wakes at noon and walks around in a dream.

But then the trade to Boston and the fall.
Olympia begins its long decline.

The only hope is tear the building down.

And even in those heady shoulder-hoisting days,
something darker seemed to bide its time.
Despite the accolades, the nights were bad, his body
ached and his head went wild, the frightful hell of waking up
at 3 a.m. He changed his nooks and crannies like a cat.
His flaring moods that set the team on edge.

That missed first shot.
That bouncer.

Once you sensed the possibilities.

Long Memories

The wind blows down from Canada. The traffic
in sleet coming off the water, the taxi creeps up Grande River
toward the Olympia. Brick bank. Brick church, St Leo's
on the right. Brick stadium. Brick neighbourhood
you'd never blow down.

Dineen and I, passing beneath the Adoring Gaze
out half the night with an afternoon game, the door-bolts
and brick stuck with white, the Virgin in her alcove
over the door. "Plastered," mutters Dineen.
"And Montreal in town with memories." Reardon,
exacting prophet, splintering Gardner jaw as he'd promised.
And something nasty brewing with Lindsay and deadly Richard,
the brawl in Montreal, then trouble again on the train.
This an ancient game with ancient laws.

All morning I tried to sleep in a blasting wind.
House of straw. House of sticks. A wise man builds a house
of bricks. But we grew up in Winnipeg, Ukrainians, Jews and Poles,
in clapboard homes that needed paint. They leaned with the wind
and reeked of cabbage and beets. Kaczynski's father bent
with the wind as well and anglicized the family name.
"Hey," Kaczynski flipped his cigarette away.
"At least I get a name in the papers now."
East Kildonan's only goal, number 12
from number 6 and J. McKay.

Near the Olympia's entrance, the crowd moves quick,
like someone poked an anthill with a stick.
"Whole city goin' to da hockey game," the driver, inching
forward, grumbles. "Black folk, we don't care for games of ice
and snow," he looks around and grins. We sit and listen to the wipers
as we wait, *yes no yes no.* He stares at the massive building,
nodding, as if he's figured the way to breach the walls.
Over the entrance way, the famous arched
window, before they boarded it up.

Ukrainian Bones

(i) *the Winnipeg hair*

Combing it up like Charlie Rayner then,
New York's "custodian of the twine," swooping it
high in the front and over and out with it wet, the Winnipeg
quick-set, 30 below. His waiting friends with similar promontories.
Thin jackets. Backs to the wind like a choir.

You'd see the hair flash past above the boards,
big waves in the sun, one breaking into the clear, the others
in sleek pursuit. Looked like the ocean rolling in.

(ii) *spectators*

Seventeen and off to the six bright cities.
Those twelve-dollar shoes that caught his eye in Galt
on the way, two-toned, their breezy angle of display. *Spectators.*
Shoes for those who discriminate. Well, what to make of that, catching
his image in the glass, the North End slouch, the Slavic darkness
of his eyes. Black cats on polish cans looked out at him
identically. *Shoes to make the man.*
And shielding his eyes against the window's glare,
missed, for the first time in his life,
the first spit of snow in the air.

Two bucks down, two more each week
out of the twenty they gave him. Fourteen for room
and board left six. But something must have happened
the day he wore them home—he'd let some easy ones in,
or maybe just a goalie's mood. Maybe someone nudged a friend
in passing, wise to the shoes and showy hair, the hint of Asia
in his bones. Still, he'd been so careful coming home,
those wings like an angel, surely they'd lift
his heart they looked so fine, but never
to wear them again,
not once.
And being born in 1929.

(iii) *short nights*

A taxi into the tunnel from Windsor, tapping
at tail lights dropping into the loop, up and into the scissoring
long black legs and American air. Blink by St Leo's Virgin,
her eyes cast down, concealing what she knows
of good beginnings.

Down Grande River to the Barn,
Detroit's Olympia, the sleet off the river
bricked out, the basking fans in the heat and smoke
of fat cigars. You let a soft one in you hear them
bitch and groan. *Hey bring back Lumley.*
Bring up Hall.

Not long before the hair was gone.
All of it off.
The heat and murder in his crease, he said.
The jeers and sneers was what he meant. Mouths like fish
against the glass. Spectators. Jesus. How long would you take
to hate them? *All of it off.*
And darkened his looks from lying awake,
or brooding apart in bars. The disappeared sleep, the ban
on food from home, pirogies and kasha, potatoes in heavy cream
and cheese, and sleep, oh sleep, and the haunting eyes
of Richard, this time charging out into the fray
and catching the son of a bitch before he could shoot.
Or choking over the coached apology, that weasel reporter
he'd pinned to the wall with a skate.

All of which emphasized his Ukrainian bones.

But man, that wave in the days of his rampant expectation,
man, you could have surfed that thing.

Different Ways of Telling Time

(i)   *last minute of play*

Four-faced, the clock sees everywhere.
Dead centre over the ice, it hangs from chains.
The players glance up, exchange a word, a sideward
look—less than a minute to go. They know time's rough
and tumble. Space and time, that's where they live,
arcs and angles, a quick move into open ice.
Their flashy physics.

Spectacles shift and glitter behind the glass.
Maybe someone they know but they never look
at the crowd. They're at the bench to hear the plan—
"Boys, you get a bounce here, things can happen fast."
Left out on the ice—they might as well be
on the moon—both goalies eye the clock,
one's for zero, the other likes infinity,
but things can change.

Get going clock.
Slow down slow down.

No one in the building likes time's pace.

(ii)   *you could drift out here forever*

Jesus, here we go.
Seventh game and seconds left to overtime.

Talk's over at the glass, the captains
waved away. The referee holds four fingers up
and folds his arms, four seconds he wants put back
on the clock. *Son of a bitch*, an old defender
sags against the boards. Still, imagine the power,
to kick time's arse like that.

(iii)   *sudden death*

The light begins to fade. The cat wants out.
The hours to game-time leak away.
A hint of green pushes into the woods on the long par five
behind the house. I watch the cat sharpen up on a favourite stump.
She yawns and stretches out to twice her length, then leisurely,
she makes her way toward the trees.

Driving into the city, the traffic's heavy,
creeping along in a cloud of exhaust. Stop and go.
The radio low. Country songs, warnings about the snow
coming down from Canada. Clutch in clutch out and drift in dreams
of accidents and overtime. Blink and you're done, a dead man
or worse, a radio joke until four in the morning.

(iv)   *ice time*

The guys arrive as if at random intervals,
lay out their gear, lucky shirt, same skate first,
same old jokes about my liniment, *Jesus,*
Ukey, lose that shit why don't you?
Roll their eyes and tiptoe by.
Check the clock and tape my own stick,
thank you, heel to toe, no wrinkles, tape the ankles.
Time to go out and get loose, guys in twos and threes
at home on ice, tucking pucks lazily under the crossbar.
Same old talk, someone you got to slow down,
a glance where he's talking it up
with his own guys.

Here's the house where I live, I can't say no.
Howe and Lindsay's eyes on me. Pronovost, tough
as a bag of batteries, slaps my pads. I see myself as I pass
in the glass, pick up the look from the other side, a nice pair
of knees that edge apart as I go by. I get a whiff of ice
and something in me starts alive. I take
a few shots, catch and flick, feeling
quick, clank behind me,
lucky too.

Then back inside and bedlam now. Adams
flapping but I don't hear. *Holy Mary, don't let me
fall on my face tonight.* I try to loosen a pad, my shaking
hand so bad *Jesus Jesus.* Tommy Ivan shoves in beside me,
knowing he needs to settle me down. New cufflinks on.
Knocks my stick for luck I'm nodding but Mother of Christ
I'm dying inside, can't keep still now everybody wants to go,
the clatter and chatter, rockers, talkers. "Gotta have this one.
Gotta have it, guys." This was where we'd bellow out
some raunchy song when we were young, scare
the bejesus out of everyone. "Nice neighbourhood like this,"
they'd say. "Who let the bloody DPs in?" Tommy drums
a rhythm on my leg—I watch his moving hand,
distracted by the veins and lines that make the hand
a miracle, an acrobat, a thief. *Gotta have it, guys.*
I brace for the roar at the end of the tunnel.
"Give me a hand here, Tommy, tuck that in, that—look
that bloody strap." Then *bang* the door and Jesus here we go,
someone shouts those words I love and dread, I hear
them all my life—*Let the goalie go first.*

(v) carpe diem

They yammer at the press in towels
and the present tense—"So I see Goldie sneaking in
and what I think, I think . . . "

I flick the water from a blade. The living
moment's where they ply their trade, *you get a chance
you make it count.* They like where time gets in your face
and open ice where you can really fly, or close-in battle
when the sticks get high, the action hot and heavy
as a leg draws up the sheet and slowly
opens out, *my living Christ.* They swing behind the net,
glancing up to find a gap, an open man, they like the crowd
up on their feet, the bodies piling on, the heft
and taste of women overhead.

"So I see Goldie sneaking in, I'm thinking, man,
if I can just draw Lumley to the post then slip it back

to him, but holy jumpin' don't let this one get away.
You get your chance, you better make it count.
I guess I just get lucky, Fred."

I wipe the other blade and smile.
Seems a neighbourhood I know from long ago.

    (vi)   *big river*

Stirring in the dark from ache to ache, crabbing
after scraps of sleep. Outside, the muffled quiet says the snow
has come. I love the city softly locked.
Let it snow forever.

I watch her shoulder's gentle rise and fall,
like she's floating on the water.
Her back's a miracle, so long and smooth
and brown, and there the jut of hip in envied sleep.
I trace a nail along her spine. Where has she been to get
so brown? What was she saying as I fell asleep?—The smell
of smoke from open fires, barking dogs and swimming out
into the harbour in the dark. Drifting off, I'd felt her
fingers trace their path from scar to scar. *This was Watson,*
this one here, Henri Richard, and here's the night Pit Martin
cracked your mask and blackened both your eyes, this one
you can hardly see, your brother on the rink
behind your house . . .

How good was that tonight. The guys
were bouncing off the walls. Jack was grabbing
everyone—he knew we had it in us all the time. His buddies
from the press were happy too, no trouble getting anyone
to talk tonight. You hear the racket in the shower,
"What a smack, that little head fake shit . . . "
"Just a sucker punch, hey everybody
knows the guy . . ."

I don't need her clock to know the time.
I shift the arm again, but can't shake something
someone said last night—"Hey, that kid out there
in Edmonton, that gaping hole between his legs,
but man he's got the corners covered.
Ukey Ukey watch your ass."

I crab a little closer to her back.

God, how bad I need this heat.

Let's Go Dancing

Watson, at 210 then, shot like a crowbar,
lets fly from the top of the circle. Somehow I lose it,
take one full in the mouth.

Jesus. Spitting bits of tooth and blood.
Lefty's out through the gate in a flash so I know
it's not good news. Here's the worst of it, you're sick
to death of the life but worried over your job, and Lefty says,
"What bad luck, we just send Hall back out to Edmonton . . ."

The clinic and its dread utensils, the clatter
in pans, blood by the door, not mine.
"Some woman out on Grande River," the doctor says,
"she wouldn't let go of her purse, so he slashes her face,
the son of a bitch." Hums to himself as he thumbs back my lip
and murmurs it's getting to be a nasty neighbourhood.
Hums the same tune as last time, stitching my lip,
I count five on the inside, seven out, is twelve,
thinking, what's that song? "Forget the freezing," I tell him,
thinking of Lumley the night when they toss me over his sweater.
First snow in fall he's gone with the birds. "Jesus no, forget
the freezing." Twenty minutes tops, I skate back
into the roar and hammering feet of the crowd.
They love me tonight, the shits.

And I'm standing on my head out there.
I stop everything they throw at me but one. A minute
to go, the crowd's up again and gone crazy and wouldn't you
know, I even remember the song—*Is that all there is,
my friend?* Though I won't be dancing tonight,
no ice-cold beer, no inch-thick steak for me to celebrate.
Still, I'm the one with the grin, big enough gap
for a truck as Gordie says, laughing,

and Hall back in Edmonton, freezing his ass.

Next Time

Six attackers, frantic to even the score,
the rink tips, bodies piling onto me. Ferguson
hacks my bad elbow, his look says, *Here's bone for your jar.*
Hooks my feet from under me, lands on my legs. I punch
at the back of his head and get this whiff of hair cream.
All of this in silence. Nothing personal,
though there may be memories.

Flat on my back, I see Backstrom looking
for the puck. I know what's coming, what I saw them
hatching at the bench, Toe's brain going like his gum, single
economic nod. I shift and lift a pad, using Ferguson for
leverage, my sprawl a calculated disarray, my hand
a hawk leap, rips the heart from the crowd.
Backstrom bangs his stick on the ice, his curse
the one word spoken in the whole exchange.

Slowly I roll to my knees. Storey's hauling guys
off me, tossing them left and right. Something's gone
again, no feeling in the hand that holds the stick.
I see Toe behind their bench now, staring
into the rafters. Who are you talking to, Toe?
Funny, I might have been playing for him if Adams
hadn't lost his nerve—the thought of me in goal
for Montreal. Where's my own guys?
Coming out of the same corner?
Where you been boys? Kelly taps my pad
and turns towards the bench. There's that look
that makes me warm all over, says, *What do you do
with a guy from a different planet.*

Storey helps me to my feet. I see that hand as large
as my trapper, the look that says, *Hey remember the time
you called me a drunken bum?* Jesus. The baggage over the years.
Still, there's no love lost between him and Ferguson,
but a minute left, we're into no man's land.
His look says, *Next time leave it to me.*

Big Dogs (1)

More and more it takes a moment just to sort things out, sometimes even to find myself. It's dark and deep in there. You want to mark your way back, like Hansel and Gretel. You live in the moment as an athlete and a referee, but now it's mainly in my memories I spend my time. Surprising how easy to keep a kind of order there, piece of cake for someone who's been an official in four sports. Not to say I ever understood it all. Him for example. Who could ever get a handle on him? But I like how they never change, the important memories, never new details to get in the way. I travel between them easily now. I remind myself more and more of Helen, my first wife. Catholic and French Canadian, she'd drag me into old cathedrals. We'd sit in the quiet a while, then wander past the Stations of the Cross. I used to ask her which was her favourite. I liked number nine myself, those sad and waiting women by the road, a little sanity and dignity and caring in all the craziness. She'd only look at me and smile—at what, I never really knew. Sometimes, what brings you back is something happening here in the present. Bunny, in the entranceway, scraping paper off the wall. A new voice at the door. I listen to hear how she likes him.

"Oh I *knew* him." Storey looks up from wherever he's been and begins to speak again. "The number of games I worked and the kind of guy I was, I knew them all. But there was something about him, something more than just how good he was. You noticed people were always looking to see where he was or what he was doing. When I think about him, I see him head down, lazily sweeping snow from his crease. Or, late in the game, he'd be down on one knee, his eyes on the ice. His mind on God knows what." He settles back in his carved wooden chair, unfurling and furling the edge of a woollen blanket that covers his legs. "That's what you want to know about, I suppose."

Even the sound of his name says hockey to me. When he was on his game, there wasn't anyone better. And he seemed to save his best for Montreal, and me working out of here then, I saw him a lot. He nearly drove Dick Irvin out of his mind, pacing back and forth behind the Canadiens' bench, leaning close to one guy's ear then leaning close to another. After the game I'd say, Dick you gotta take it easy, one of these nights you'll have a stroke out here. "I can't help it," he says. "How the dickens do you beat the guy? He knows what you're going to do before you do it. I never see it but I

*know he's always watching me. I lie awake at night. I think my wife is
going to leave me."*

Storey listens a moment to the noises in the hall. An old front door
with stained glass panels rattling closed. A plastic bucket's hollow clunk.
The scraping at the walls again. "Well, that's a bit of a joke, me saying
that to him and it happens to me. Hey, you know what they say, how
big dogs don't live as long. Look at me—83 and rising out of my ashes
again. We live a long time in my family and I always lived the way I
played my games, hard but clean. And I've been blessed with wonderful
people around me, starting with my mother. Now I got a new hero—
she's the one who let you in. Taught me how to live all over again. Fed
me with a spoon. Showed me what the pan was for." He glances at the
door then pushes the blanket away from his legs. Here in his den, the
walls are cluttered with photographs and yellowed pages from the
papers, the shelves and mantel behind him with trophies. "That one's
him in Detroit in '52. What he did in the playoffs that year will never
be done again." He jabs his thumb over his other shoulder. "That's him
again, jawing away at some fan. That was Terry too. But I'll tell you
this about him, mister—he was a big game goalie. He was the one you
wanted when the heat was on. I've seen him use the handle of his stick
to stop the puck."

*He made me think of my football days. Big as he was and alert and
crouched like a cat, he looked more like your middle linebacker watching
everywhere, bracing himself to knock somebody down. Balance and angles,
that's what he understood. Terry was a great angle goalie, one of the first.
That's what beat him up—21 years of taking shots to the body and terrible
gear. But it was football damaged his arm, locked it like this, see, good for
holding the stick, but he could never lift it over his head. He broke it
getting tackled as a kid and wouldn't say a word for days, too frightened
to tell his mother. No football, she'd said. Sounds familiar, not much point
going up against what mine wanted either. Once he told me she was the
only one in the world who scared him. He loved the game though. He liked
to watch the Lions play in Detroit. Got into some heavy drinking with some
of their guys, I heard. Maybe football was where the crouch comes from.
Wherever, it changed the game.*

"Him and Hall and Plante. I'd of taken any one of them. Too bad you can't go talk to Plante. That guy was one of a kind. Before he played goal for Montreal, he was a catcher here in the old Quebec League— Johnny Wilson used to pitch to him. And here's Toe Blake telling him you wear a mask, you'll never find the puck at your feet. Toe didn't miss much but he missed that one. Plante and Sawchuk and Hall. After those guys, playing goal was never the same. And Bower and Worsley. There's others, Durnan, Rayner, Lumley . . . Doesn't bear thinking about, what it took to stand in there night after night, no mask, no backup, nobody else on the team with a half a clue what goalies were up against. The coaches weren't much better. Toe was one of the greatest, but the wars that him and Plante had over the mask." He shakes his head. "Well, you know who won that one in the end. Go talk to Kenny Reardon, he was there. And Eddie Shore, for goodness sakes, a great coach, but he could be a madman dealing with goalies. He hated it when they went down, even to make a save. He wanted his goalies to stay on their feet. Once he drops a noose around his goalie's neck in practice and slings the rope up over a beam. Every time the poor bugger starts to go down, Eddie jerks the rope. Me, I tried to protect them. I'd seen too many hurt and hurt bad, and I had a sense of what they were up against. The game was changing too in Sawchuk's day, everyone trying to figure out how to beat those guys. Geoffrion wailing away with his slap shot. Hull and the boys in Chicago heating the blades of their sticks and bending them under the dressing room door. Slapshots. Screen shots. Deflections. Pucks flying everywhere. You knew how hard when you heard them whack the glass. The traffic in front got heavier too, goalies getting run over, hooked and hauled down. I'd be in as quick as I could, peeling guys off them."

The scraping out in the hall moves closer now. Storey looks down at his hands again and around the walls. There's not much wallpaper showing in here, with all his clippings and photographs and shelves of trophies. "All my adult life," he says, "I've lived in this house. And I'd leave for the Forum closing that glass door so carefully . . ." He's quiet a moment, getting his thoughts back together. "I saw more than a few who buckled under the pressure of playing goal. Here in Montreal, Durnan, McNeil, Wilf Cude a bit further back, even Worsley, once he comes to know what it's like to play for a team that's expected to win. Even Plante. Some wise guy reporter makes a joke about it, calling it rubberitis. *He'd* never have to face a Bobby Hull slapshot, a puck flying at you over a hundred miles an hour. Over the years, I watched as Terry lost his way. All the anxiety, the injuries, the hard losses, the fans and papers blaming him, calling him washed up and sullen and surly. It takes its toll. Four hundred stitches in his face alone. He had trouble sleeping too because of what the years in that deep crouch did to his back. And that weird thing with his weight. They make him lose weight, then he can't get it back when he needs it. They pay more attention to that sort of thing nowadays. I blame Adams for all that. Terry had a big family too. Then his heavy drinking at the end."

Harvey and Sawchuk. You think of them together. Sad, the two of them get tagged with being booze hounds. Big men, both of them, and proud, and the best at what they did. They both had long careers, too long, and got slower and bitter over being bought and sold and treated badly by the fans and the press. Guys as good as they were, people always ask too much. There's some nasty sons of bitches up in the crowd. Any referee can tell you that.

"Harvey and Sawchuk," he says. "That funny connection too, the big trade of one for the other that never gets made when Adams gets cold feet. When it came down to it, even having Harvey, Adams doesn't want any part of facing Terry with all that firepower in front of him. So he buries him in Boston with the lowly Bruins. Goodbye Terry, Goodbye. He was never the same after that. Not as a player and not as a person. Guys in those days, they felt a loyalty to their teams. Terry trusted Jack Adams like a father. Dumping him off like that, Adams destroyed his confidence. It made him bitter. Even when Jack goes sour on Hall and brings Terry home to Detroit, he's never the same. All the shots and hits he took in all those years, they did a job on him. But getting traded away from what they had there in Detroit, that really did him in."

He sits back in his chair, the big head nodding slowly, remembering. "Tough town, Boston. They never forgave him for leaving the team like he did. Man, they spared no one. There was one guy really used to give it to me. 'Hey Storey,' he'd bellow, 'we got a town down here named after you.' And he always picked his spot. Always that same foghorn voice, that same line, but I never knew when it was coming. It wasn't linked to anything I did or said or how the game was going. But everyone in the Gardens was waiting. I'd be waiting too and sometimes it would get really late in the game and I hadn't heard anything and I'd think, thank Christ, maybe just this once, he's not here. Maybe he's dead. But sure as hell that's when you'd hear it, 'Hey Storey, we got a town in Massachusetts named after you.' Everyone would go quiet and then he'd bellow, 'Marblehead!' And the whole darn place would crack up. Even the players would look at me and grin. Same line every time but the guy just had the voice and really knew how to get under your skin. 'We got a town down here named after you.' Man, those days are gone."

He's quiet again a moment. A grey light comes in through a window. Montreal in winter. Grey light, grey days. But a briskness in the downtown streets, an intensity, especially when the Canadiens were home for a couple of games. "St Catherine's and Atwater," he looks up suddenly. An energy returns to his voice even as his face grows indistinct in the fading light. "It was always busy down there. But when you saw those words up over the Forum's doors, *Hockey Tonight*—man, they just picked up your step, even after I was out of the League. They told you life was good. They told you the woman with you was just the right one, and whichever restaurant or bar you were heading for was just the perfect place to go before the game." Storey looks back at his hands a moment, looking from one to the other, as if he were weighing something. "Well, I'm a positive guy and something tells me you might understand all that. I don't know.

Sometimes I think the trade was what did him in and sometimes I think it was something else altogether. I remember a kind of darkness in him from the start. He had a wonderful side—he could be kind and dry and humourous. Then you'd get the silences. And sudden explosions.

"Jesus that crazy question he asks me that time."

"Did I ever get him figured out? Ask me something easier."

Desperate Moves

"The greatest save I ever saw
in hockey," says Plante, waving pages of notes
in his trapper hand, the black suit too tight and the tie
too narrow, emphasizing an angular face and a startling
inelegant sprawl as he tries in his chair to show Ward Cornell
just how Sawchuk, flat on his back in a pileup
in front, puts a pad high in the air
to save the game,

as Terry himself turns up. He's come
straight from the ice in his gear for a rare interview,
easing himself and his leaden pads towards an awkward chair.
Cables, tables, precarious lights. Disaster a stumble away,
he knows about that.

He's careful too with Plante's enthusiasm,
shrugs off the compliments—the guys were clearing
rebounds, the forwards picking up their man.
Asked about the save, he looks away,
"I stuck up a leg," as if to say like anyone would.
"He puts one on the ice it's in. You know yourself,
Jacques, it's better to be lucky than good."
Plante resists a cozy acquiescence like a monk.
He seems too open, too unguarded for a goalie. The heart
of matters is what he wants to wade into, but this is Hockey Night
in English Canada. His catching hand comes up to make
a point, to ask about the sudden drop in weight,
over 200 pounds to 165 in a year, the trade, the brutal
Boston press, the train in the night to Detroit. But Terry
steers the questions off into a corner. "You do what you have
to do. You know I've always admired you, Jacques,
down at the other end."

Plante sits back, unsatisfied, and Ward murmurs
something inert about grit or momentum.

You see the goaltenders glance at one another,
the only moment in the interview that their eyes meet.
The silent exchange is arresting.
They know each other's subtlest movements
in their sleep, but they're not accustomed to being
so close. You wonder what they might have said
to one another, left alone, but up this close
it's better to keep side-on.
That's the message from Terry at least.

"So when you saw Keon wide open," says Plante,
"what you made was a desperate move."

"That's it, Jacques," Sawchuk says, all in one motion
detaching his mike and rising up out of the ill-considered chair,
"that's all it was."

III. TWO GOALIES GOING FISHING IN THE DARK

This way, oh turn your bows,
Akhaia's glory,
As all the world allows –
Moor and be merry.

> – Homer's Song of the Sirens,
>   *The Odyssey*, trans. Robert Fitzgerald

INDIA BEER

Presents

THE OFFICIAL

PROGRAMME

AND

PHOTOGRAPH

OF

NATIONAL HOCKEY LEAGUE

BOSTON BRUINS

1956 NEWFOUNDLAND TOUR

A WARM WELCOME TO THE
BOYS FROM BOSTON FROM
THE BREWERS OF

INDIA BEER

Night Crossing in Ice

We locked up the cars in North Sydney
and looked at the sea, grey and uninviting, nothing
like inland ponds or lakes that we knew. "You could sink forever,"
someone murmurs. Close cloud, the colour says bad mistake.
Something on the beach attracting gulls. Wreckage
and rock. The start or end of things,
who could say?

We went aboard the *William Carson* in the dark,
the wind's kiss like a lost wife. Gulls on the waterfront
sheds looked away as we sailed. Nine or ten hours
the crossing if the weather holds, but we barely
get into the bar when the fun begins—
pitch and roll and
bang Jesus Christ the bow riding up
and hammering down we grab at anything,
lifted and dangled, our bodies hopeless, recognizing nothing
of this motion. *Porpoising, boys, that's what we calls it
here. Guaranteed, she'll be a memorable night.*

Who could call this heaving darkness home?
Who'd go out of his house in this for a game of hockey?
All night long a locker door slams shut like someone
raging, looking for the one way out. Up and
hold on the crest and
down with a bang and bang that
bloody door, then deep in the night a grinding, inches
from my ear, as if we were into a depth of animals. *Nothing
but ice, my love,* I hear a passing voice in the corridor, *pans and a bit
of slob, we sees all we wants of that in the spring.*

Solid Ground

If it hadn't been for the fog and the bad crossing,
he might have been up on deck and seen the weedy rocks
ease by, the gulls like moody frontier guards.
And high in the wind on the naked headland,
the first signs of human habitation, Bruce Arena,
bolted fast to the rock and windowless facing the water
on three sides. In such a country, he might have pondered
the wisdom of letting ice indoors or knocking any man down.
A shiver might have been the chilly April air, or a thought
of taking the weather end of the rink as the wind
shook the walls and the waves climbed over one another,
eager to smash the building into the sea. In a lull, he might have
heard what the wind heard, or the housebound, keeping an ear
to the racket up on the hill, the roar at a big-time save
or a flattened opponent, some fool who came waltzing in
with his head down. Under the hill, too close
to the water, a few scoured graves.
Where visiting players ended up, no doubt.

If it weren't for the fog and his general gloom
heading on by train—the seating cramped, and there it was
in a local paper, Glenn Hall in Terry's sweater (looking a little green
around the gills himself) while he, Terry, dangled over the edge
of the known world—he might have noticed a startling bit
of erotic topography just west of Port Aux Basques,
a most distinctive pair of conical hills, ample and comforting,
the perfect suggestion of a woman reclining.

What world have I come to, he might have wondered,
if it hadn't been that his mind was miles away
on what he'd always thought was solid ground, St Leo's
and the Olympia, built with identical brick, the hat-check girl
at Joe Bathay's, the blotch on that sweater Lefty had never been
able to wash away. Under the hills a silver pond flashed by
unseen. This was a country that could show you things,
but you had to be in a half-decent mood,
and looking.

Dinner at the Priest-House

for Al Pittman

They lean to Montreal and Boston, Catholic teams.
The trade from Detroit they see as deliverance, hardly the fall
from grace that Protestant papers call it. Father Kelly,
who played with Flaman, invited us all
but I went alone in the end.
The first questions follow the prayer,
"Don't the Bruins stick together?" What do I
hear? Disappointment or nose out of joint? Forks
pause in the clerical air. The room's like ours at the local
hotel. There's no one's place or favourite plate.

"And what we hear all about the Rocket and Lindsay,"
one plasters a roll with butter, "do they really hate each other?"
"And the Wings and Montreal, is it true they have to put a dining car
between them on the train?" And hadn't I heard about the wars
in St John's—St Bons against the Guards and Bishop Feild?
"Oh, that was hockey in its glory days!"
An older priest, with an air of his work being done,
lingers over something said earlier—"Only six goalies
in all the League? That might have a man
looking over his shoulder."
Younger throats clear in alarm. Something
lemon appears in front of me. The talk resumes
of local talent and who might catch us by surprise tonight.
Father Kelly only smiles. He hasn't said much since he found me
alone in the church. Not where you'd expect your two-time all-star,
crumpled under a dark Madonna. I'd heard him pause behind me
then move a little away. The priest at the head of the table
smiles when I find a place to mention her. "Our Virgin
on the Humber, she'd be from another time and a different order.
Too quirky for my taste." Saucers clink. Murmurs of assent.
"Some unschooled local, wouldn't you think? Goodness.
That river looking like a serpent in her hair.
The eyes quite clearly with a hint of petulance.
And why would anyone want to paint
a Virgin without the Saviour?"

Father Kelly says nothing. Proud of his former skills,
they'd placed him next to me. "The road not taken, Joe,"
says the older priest in another pause.
Only Father Kelly smiles.

I stare at the molten light in an unused spoon.
Not a crowd for second thoughts, it's easy to see. One,
left-handed, cuts his meat in an awkward way,
and my heart sinks.

Signs of Recognition

The kid's by the boards where Gardner
glides to the line for "The Queen." He's got his Boston
cards laid out on his lap, and an older brother who's brought him
to the game. They'd be the age of my brother and me when he died.
April 1956. No TV out in the icebergs yet to know
who's who. His eyes jump suddenly. "George!" his voice
breaking into the rising and half-begrudged hush,
"George! That's Cal Gardner!!"

You hear a buzz as the anthem ends and laughter
in the building—"George that's Cal Gardner!"
Grown men who need to let their own excitement loose.
Faces press forward to hear and pass it on, maybe mend a fence
in the process, or lean precariously close to a pair of legs
of local fame. Our guys glance around as if waking
to something. They take in the ice, too clear for ice indoors,
the bad light, and look up into the rafters, so close, goddamn,
you want to duck your head. And look how the bolts are furred
with frost, "Man, there's a memory." One by one, they look around,
half-expecting friends or a favourite uncle warming his hands on a cup
of coffee. "Tell me the last time you looked at the crowd."

And Cal, with his carved and elegant jaw,
winks and turns to the kid with a two-gun salute
that lights up the eyes you barely see over the boards
and starts it all over again, the ripple of joy rolling outward
and down to the ends of the rink and around and meeting the first
coming back like waves colliding under a cliff with others rolling in,
the whole building seeming to rock and sway, the way
even a big boat might in such giddy water.

That's Cal Gardner. The older brother
bends to hide a smile and Cal—you could have knocked us
flat with spit—he grins and gives him that little shake
of the head you see here that says as much as needs
to be said. How'd he pick that up so easily?

Fair Trade

I skate out to talk to their goalie at centre ice,
the game half done and the score about 20 to nothing.
The guys put four past him real quick, the building still
buzzing over Mackell and the move he makes on this guy
at the net and how he had those two poor buggers
working their tails off, trying to catch him.
Heads down, legs pumping like they're skating
for their lives—it's only an exhibition game, but who
can tell what dreams awaken in your head?
The crowd was wild as they hit the blue line, Mackell
out in front but the pair of them gaining, the crowd
gone crazy, driving them harder, girls who'd never give them
a glance downtown, the teachers and mill bosses' wives
in a frenzy urging them on, when Mackell reaches
absently back with one hand (I knew this was coming)
and tucks in the tail of his sweater.

My eyes take in the goal pads, stitched and patched,
the taped-up toes of his skates, the battered trapper where
he's got the puck Mackell puts past him, jerking
him out of his jockstrap. He shakes his head
like it's all a blur, what happened there.
I could say you need to see the shot
before it leaves the stick, but he'd look at me
as if I had two heads. I start hauling off my sweater
and say, instead, "How'd you like to play
goal for the Boston Bruins?"

Alarmed, he lifts an eyebrow,
glancing around at the crowd and his bench
and his two guys hanging over the boards trying to catch
their breath. "Well b'y," he says, and I see he's thinking it over,
"I wouldn't say no, if you'd like to play
for the Corner Brook All-Stars."

Nothing but Moonlight Here

Terry looks out at me, pointing just inside the post
as I was next. That roused the boys for a joke
or two about goalies together. I lumbered in like some old
woods-horse deep in snow or a man balled up with the weight
of the world. I knew what the trouble was, divided loyalties.
I tried to blank out who's in goal, with a chance
to close the gap.

Did I mention they put four past me real quick?
Undressed me in front of everyone I know.

After the game and half a dozen drinks
we went out onto *my* ice—two goalies going fishing
in the dark. "So where's the lake?" he looks around, coming out
of the woods, nothing but moonlight here, nothing but snow.
"You're standing on it," I said.

I showed him how you feel with your line
for the bottom. He sat, not saying much and catching less,
but a hole in the ice at night is a dangerous thing, and he told me
a thing or two about the life I wouldn't mention here.
I was after rubbing places where I'd taken shots,
surprising myself with some I'd stopped and crazy things
had started creeping into my head. Over a snow-covered lake,
a moon can be mischievous. But slowly a chill crept into my bones
and more than once I thought about my wife, and how she'd come
hammering back to bed in the cold and crush against my heat.
And how she'd warm her hands between my legs, the way
she liked to fall asleep. And my rabbit snares
in the woods. I thought about those.
And Mad Dog Lake and up in the wind after birds
with a friend or coming on caribou tracks
in an early snow.

Yes, it was four they tucked in behind me
before the shine was even off the ice.

And then I missed that open side he left
for me, bounced it off the post with everybody looking on.
Foolish to be so fine in goalie gear. Out on the lake
that night I got free of a lot of foolishness
I wouldn't mention here.

Ineptness and geography.
I doubt there's many find salvation where they hope.

Cardinal Sin

He falls down twice on his way to the net. I sense
the crowd lean forward, ready to leap. What's this about?
Is this what it all comes down to after Detroit, a little goalie show
for the fans? Waiting at center ice to take their shots, his team-mates
circle nervously, flipping snow at friends in the stands.
What wouldn't they give to put one past me,
here in front of the home crowd.

Get up for Jesus sake, I want to shout. The crowd
makes me nervous—they're not surprised by this, the second time
he half goes down, I glance to see how many yet to go.
Cardinal sin. The stick explodes like a catapult,
whacking the puck past my ear into the goal.
The crowd erupts. Close. Too close.
A flinch from taking out an eye. Notes to clarify
a bright but short career—*He made the trip to Newfoundland
when Boston missed the playoffs once again. Regan gave him
25 dollars a game. He had a large family to feed.*

"Ger-ald! Ger-ald!" The crowd begins to chant,
a kind of mocking adulation, and I go after him with my stick.
Stupid. I know who I'm angry at. What stops me cold is that look
in his eyes, the same glazed look I see in Richard when he
puts one in. The fire gone briefly out.
An almost-sheepishness at how fierce he'd been.

"Sorry, Terry," their goalie comes over to sort it out.
Says the guy's a little different, and talks around it later
out on the lake. Says he keeps track of his goals in practice
and grew up with the Brothers in St John's. One thing he knows
is how to put the puck in the net. He's deadly on his knees.
Goalies here don't like you to knock him down.

"Jesus, Gerald." Gently he bends to help him up.
"They told you keep the puck down. It's just supposed to be
a bit of fun, b'y."

String and Bones

was

"Part of the show, hey? We all get a penalty shot
to try to close the gap? But you know how nervous you'd be,
going one-on-one against the greatest ever."

"Oh, Gerald. Well, he'd be the man to put one in."

"My son, I won't forget it. Falling down he whacks a bullet
right at Sawchuk's head. He had to be quick."

"What went on in Gerald's head? Well, who might help you
there I couldn't say. What went through mine was everyone I knew
in the world was there, including a girl from Curling
I was moony over then."

"Just a shot, you know, nothing special. I'd say
Sawchuk let it in on purpose."

"That was my own bad luck I get the middle shift
at the mill that week so never saw either game, but Gerald
had a good job with the railroad and one of the Bruins didn't make
the train, I wouldn't like to say his name, but Gerald arranged
a place that night on a pulp and paper train,
something not just anyone could do."

"Oh yes, he had his well-known temper.
Once in Detroit he whipped a skate at some reporter's head,
another time he goes right up over the screen to get at some fan.
Imagine seeing that in all his glory coming at you."

"A fluke is what I'd have to say. Why Terry took such exception,
I wouldn't know who you could find to tell you now."

"Went after him? I don't remember that.
But Gerald, he wasn't nothing then but string and bones."

(ii) *isn't*

"So you're the man who scored on Terry Sawchuk."

I find him in Lewisporte, living in the cottages.
I take a table in the small cafe where I can see the water.
"Oh he'll talk to you about hockey," the waitress brings
me bad coffee, "just give him half an opening."
Waiting, I glance at some notes I'd made that morning
on the pier, things I wanted to know. I thought of how warm
it was out on the water where I'd talked with a man and his son
on their boat about the way the fish were.

Larger than I'd expected, he arrives in a pickup,
red or maybe it was blue, looking a little at bay. He settles
his eyes on me, the only customer. I hadn't planned to say what
I said as he stood in the door. I see his eyes well up.

"Greatest moment of my life," he says.

None of this is on the tape, which begins with a clatter
of spoons and the waitress on the phone. "Half the town
was there, my son. Don't be getting on about it
being my imagination." She lays the telephone down
to fill our cups, eyeing Gerald as he checks the sugar top
for local jokers. She looks at me as if we were hopeless,
cut from the same cloth as whoever was waiting
to finish defending himself. She sighs and goes back
to her cigarette and the phone.

He pulls his coffee closer and begins. Yes the train.
And yes the game. Staring down into the cup he holds
in both hands. "Maybe he did come after me,
but he was only kidding. Yes, he did say
something. Just like it was yesterday."

Long silence, looking out over the water,
then he turns to me. "He said, 'How come a guy with the shot
you got isn't up with us in the NHL?'"

Clobie Collins

You're like a bunch of cattle. They can sell you or trade you
and kick you out when they want to.
               – Terry Sawchuk, CBC radio interview

(i)

A jot in the margin, *hide him*
down in the codfish and rocks. Last place you'd look
for *blinding speed,* the latter phrase you come across in all
the early assessments. Because Montreal at the time was deep
in talent, Richard, Richard and Moore et al., and Backstrom
coming on. Because he was black and this was 1956,
Jack Robinson notwithstanding.
"Doesn't he come from somewhere down there
anyway?" And on to the following item in the reconditioned air,
the indirect light. Oh to play the distribution game you want
your walnut panels, the reassuring glow
that rosewood gives.

(ii)

Amos and Andy. That was it back then
with blacks in Newfoundland. "He was big," they say
with widening hands, as if describing the dream fish.
"Nobody messed with him on the ice. Like lightning, buddy,
going up the boards. He'd fend you off like a bit of fluff
and cut in around you." The buzz in rinks and bars,
for and against. So quick to hit his stride
and women said little, but seemed distracted by his dark flame,
his pitches of mood—he'd drive to the net, then soft as the sheets
off the line they loved to press against their face,
he'd float back to centre, half sheepish
in his team-mates' mauling.

Blinding speed. You think about what that
means. It lifts you from yourself to see an animal

or someone that you love in headlong flight.
Legs pounding at their limit, unapologetic, almost
comical. You sense a bluer sky, a spring song in the rowdiness
of crows, something in a daughter's laugh that says it's
okay, let her go. You sense a quiet in the runner
after, a place to ease back into.

    (iii)

Which might account for the subsequent note
in the same tight hand, *losing a step.*
You say it first yourself as a joke. Looking back, how little
sleep he must have managed on the road. You hear the stories.
Long winter nights and far-apart lights, how many invitations
for a few drinks, how many white valleys, all but the one
you'd expect he wanted most. *Losing a step.*
We make our little jokes about it but you know
it would have closed the file on him.

What lingers is his love of endless nights
and his seeming unawareness of what set him apart,
his colour and velocity. There's a story a former linemate loves
to tell of his saying goodbye to the girls at the dressing room door.
"You be watching for me out there," he says.
"You be looking for number six."

A little joke as epitaph, but whose? You wonder
how much he meant, or whether he said it at all. Oh memory.
You want to watch it carefully. Like skating on the bay
in spring, you want to watch the darker spots
and go like stink.

The Swan-House

Glynmill Inn, Corner Brook, April 1956

McKenney and me looking down at the frozen
pond below the hotel. Open ice and a wind behind,
there's a memory. A catwalk out to a building
under the bank, pines that angle sharply up
the slope. A town of slopes and streams
and streets that amble from door to door like nosy dogs.
Two boys in rubber boots approach, the bigger one gives us
a little shake of his head. "Where's d' b'ys gone, hey?
Where's Terry Sawchuk to?" The younger one
gapes at the scars on my face as I turn.
"He's gone home," I say.

That single complicit shake of the head—
half greeting, half grimace—*yes fucked again*
it might say, or *you wouldn't believe what they're wanting
now*, the ones who own your ass, you understand. Mister
This or the Honourable That. The suits.
The stink of good cigars.

"Seventeen games in nineteen days," McKenney
murmurs, looking up a leaden sky, "twenty bucks a game
and the bus late again."

And Hall wins last night in Toronto, a waiter
lets us know. A year ago to the day it's me against Montreal
in the finals, and Adams, the bastard, mugging it up
for the press—"What d' ya think of my boy now?"
Armlock of affection on my head and all
the while he's dreaming headlines,
Sawchuk to Boston in Blockbuster Deal.
Trader Jack Shakes up the Hockey World.

McKenney says, "That's him, kid, he's just a joker,
give him what you got there." I scrawl my name with a bitten
piece of pencil and we stand in the wind looking down

at the house in the ice. "Dere's swans in the summer,"
the older one tells us, "somebody puts 'em inside
when d' pond freezes over." Cinder-block walls,
half green, half white, like rinks I been looking at all my life.
I think of them down in the dark and how everyone
loves to let you know what nasty buggers swans
can be. I wish them an early spring
and a happy forgetfulness.

Jesus, yes, and let one of those yapping mutts
forget himself for a moment and wade
a little too far out into the pond.

A Little Story on Himself

(i)

Gerry Regan tells this little story
on himself: What with Toppazzini's ear infection,
Laycoe's father getting sick, and wives on the phone
to him wanting the husbands home, the ranks were getting thin.
He'd had to dress in Grand Falls himself just to have another
body on the bench. He'd taken a lap or two to try
and get the cobwebs out and floated one in toward Terry
when he saw the boys had turned away to try to hide their grins—
Mohns had heard the Grand Falls players by their bench,
"B'ys, I tell ya we can give these guys a game.
Look at number ten—'e can barely
stand up on 'is skates."

(ii)

Toppazzini had been left behind in Corner Brook to heal. The word
was he was living like a king, women coming to visit him up in the
hospital during the day, bringing jam jams and pie and giving his neck
and shoulders a bit of a rub, then the men coming after their shift at
the mill, sitting around his bed telling stories. There was one—he
couldn't remember it all, but wouldn't forget the line it ended with,
"Who da Christ is heavin' dem goddam rocks on me roof?"

Even Terry seemed to loosen up a little. "That night in Bay Roberts,"
says Regan, "I can see him under that umbrella in the rain. We talked
a lot together on that trip, both of us being separate in a sense. He
was intense—that's what I remember most. And moody, sure, and
contradictory. You try to work him out like one of those crossword
puzzles he was always at. You get stumped and go on to another clue,
looking for the one word to unlock it all. In hindsight, I suppose
alcohol and women played their part. The spoils of war and all." He
sits a moment, quiet, then says, "He talked about his wife and kids a
lot." His hand open out philosophically. "We're all a bit of a mystery,
don't you think?"

He reaches for some cake his wife brought in with tea. "I remember late one night on the train, he slips in beside me seeing I'm not asleep and says he's been thinking he should be getting a little more than everyone else since it was mainly him who drew the crowds. Also he was taking too many shots." Regan looks around his Bedford living room, and out the window at the sailboats in the sun. He points out a novice race in the chaos of boats on the Basin. Too subtle to figure out, a gentleman's game, all the protocol of getting the boats around the buoys without a collision and total confusion.

"How could I argue? I gave him an extra five dollars a game." He looks at me quickly. "That's what he asked for. The rest were sound asleep at the time, so nobody knew." Then he adds after a moment, "I guess when you think of it, nobody knows it still." And seems amused at keeping such a secret all these years.

Colour in This Country

One by one, they came out of the bar in their gear,
the night's opponents. Talking together and joking, they passed
in front of our bus like young men at the front, their days
reduced to frivolity and disaster.

One or two stole a glance at us as they crossed
the road on their skates and struggled up an icy slope.
You recognized the hunched and terrible pace of expeditions
pushing toward the Poles. Bracing themselves, they'd haul up
those behind by their sticks, slipping and flopping about.
One went flat on his ass, giving them all
a good laugh. Everything, it seemed,
was opposition. White was having it out
with black, ice blocked the harbour, winter froze
the pipes and jammed the doors. You sensed a sparing use
of colour in this country. You'd get a splotch of it here and there,
a memorable blouse in a lounge, a clock promoting rum,
the local team in its colours taking to the ice.

The bar was where they gathered to have a drink
and change. "Jesus, how civilized can you be?"
someone said half to himself, wiping steam from the window.
As if to something said from inside, one of the last out the door
turned to look back. We watched as he hobbled back in
then, laughing, hurried after the others up into the trees.

Years later, after a famous catastrophe at sea,
I came across an old photograph of sealers on the ice.
I was in for the elbow again, the season over and white the colour
of spring for me as well. There would have been joking, I knew,
helping each other over the difficult parts. The joking done,
there would have been warnings, then grapplings
and shouts at the widening gap in the end.

I thought of the guy who came out of the bar
at the end, and what he'd gone back for, the last of his drink
perhaps, a little message in a kiss, or an old fellow's hope
they wouldn't let us make them look like fools,
and I wondered what difference it made in the end.
My own mood was darkening.
Everything seemed to be splitting away.
In the photograph, all you could really see were shapes
curving darkly into a white that might have been
the page's nothingness.

Bay Roberts

(i) *let the goalie go first*

Strange mix, the low-tide odour in the air
and damp of all our gear we can't get dry, but nothing's
what we're used to since our coming here. Someone wonders
how things went tonight in Detroit, and look at us on a yellow bus
and tons of floating ice between. Still, you feel a nagging
sense there's something that we know here too.

The guys squeeze into narrow seats, awkward
in their gear and overshoes. What's next we're thinking,
why would they take us to change in a school? Scattered lights
along the road, the mist above a choppy evil sea.
The driver drops into a lower gear and up we struggle
into a dwarfish tangle of trees. "We might be in friggin Japan,"
someone breaks the silence, wiping at his window. Nervous laughter
as we hook a rut. We know we're into a different country,
the stacked up wood and sawdust everywhere, the tilt
of everything toward the sea. "Boys," says Flaman,
peering at the glow behind the trees, "I'd say
we're playing in the great outdoors tonight."

A moon where the clock should be. A wind
bringing tears to your eyes as you raced up the ice.
It wasn't as though we didn't have the memories.
Regan looks away as if to say no one told him.
"Holy cow, the woods are alive," Boivin says. "Look,
the trees are moving down the hill." The shadows come
closer, then lift and plunge in the light by the boards.

The door flaps open right in front of me. "It's only
the b'ys cuttin' trees," says the driver. "The wind's from the east,
you won't be sorry for having some shelter tonight." Glumly, we sit
looking into the dark, unwilling to leave the comfort of heat.
The mist rolls down through the glow from the rink,
we glimpse the faces looking at us from the trees.
Someone says, *Hey, let the goalie go first.*

(ii) *east wind*

"Good night," said a voice in the trees
as if the game were done and we could all go home.
When they pulled aside the boughs to let us in, the waiting crowd
stood up and cheered. You felt a little foolish
wearing shoes.

The ice was getting soft, *sishy*, they said,
but it ought to hold up for an hour or so.
You heard the sound of moving water everywhere.
Someone beside me said what would any of these guys
know about ice. We glanced away, embarrassed by their gear,
the mismatched socks and dreadful skates. Then the sleet
came sideways out of the night and I'd forgotten how
I hated lacing skates in the cold. You heard the moaning
and bitching on the bench, when Flaman, our captain,
sniffs at the air and looks at us. "Boys," he says,
"I like the feel of things, the happy crowd,
the smell of spruce and wood-smoke in the air
and half of their team inviting us over for drinks."

Mackell gets everyone up on their feet from the start,
going end to end with the puck, then circling back and taking
it in all over again. You hear the rising buzz of disbelief.
It's a bit of a dream for them as well—until tonight,
they've only known us on the radio.
Their players go after the puck but all together
and turn to find it up the ice, tucked neatly into their net.
They glance at one another, thinking what's their part
in all of this. Slowly, they skate to centre ice,
and you see the little grins begin, as if they're seeing
the situation now—another close place and impossible odds.

Down in the dark alone, my mind drifts back
to Michigan. I see the newly flooded Olympia ice
and hear the crowd as Hall brings out the team. While here
my sweater's white with sleet and there's an uproar
in the dark as Boivin sits on both referees.

Then Flaman brings that lady's umbrella
out of the stands. "Gotta look after your goalie," he says,
looking to see how I'm taking it all tonight.

They must have had sixty guys out for the game,
four different teams crowding onto their bench until it turns
into a free-for-all at the end—they all tumble onto the ice
and the Bruins go sit on the boards or up in the crowd.
Their man in front with the puck pulls up just out of reach
and it's hard to say which is the worst of a goaltender's dreams,
the laughter welling out of the stands, or fifty-nine
sons of bitches looking for a loose puck.
"What are you doing?—Shoot the goddamned thing!"
I shout. "Not so fast my buddy, my darlin',"
he grins and drops his gloves, baring a pair of split
and battered fists, one with a program in it,
the other, a pen.

"Can we boys have y'r autograph?"

(iii) *Sea View Lounge*

"He keeps to himself," an old man beside me says,
his ancient hands on the table. I look to see Terry alone
with a beer in a corner, smoking in silence.
Around the stove, the stories grow louder
and more familiar. "Bay Roberts? Bay *Roberts?*"
says Gardner. "We thought you were sayin' Bay *Rabbits.*
By God, we might be home in Boston." And hadn't I forgotten
what a wood stove gives a room, with sleet at the windows and wind
at the door. And lord, the steam from the pots and smells coming
out of the bowls, pea soup with doughboys, the pies and beans
and bottled moose and gravy ladled over fresh-baked bread.
And cheers as Gardner and Heinrich shove back
in the line, looking for more flipper pie.
Here's to the Boston Bruins,

their captain raises a glass, *and bloody decks to 'en.*
Cheers all around, the bottles turned up and banged down
and the laughter grows louder. "A sealers' toast," the old man
says to me, "there's two at least will be off to the ice
in the morning."

A head turns to Terry now
and again, a beer appears at his elbow.
Why had I brought the umbrella out of the crowd?
"Part of the show," I'd said, "you got to look after your goalie,
boys." But that was just your mumbo-jumbo for the press.
He could be trouble, the papers said after the trade,
he could be one surly son of a bitch.
Maybe so, I wouldn't say no, but he was the horse
we rode the whole season. And something was coming clear
to us that week in Newfoundland—we were done
in Boston being doormats, and we knew
who had shown us how to win.
Why had I brought him that ladies' umbrella?
I was captain then. Somebody had to say something.

Absently, I trace the scars and burns on the table.
"Too many shots," I look at the weathered face and say,
"too many shots and goalies always take the blame."
I stare at the bent and swollen fingers resting
near mine on the comfortable wood.
"There's hard ways to make a living in the world," I say.
"Oh, my sonny boy," he says. The bottle trembles,
moving toward his tightened lips.

Narrow Gauge

Stopped in a silent white country, not far
from Gallants, they said, struck a moose or snow
on the tracks. A caustic rum went around. "Central heating,"
said one of the locals and dealt another hand. Up ahead,
the locomotive, muffled in the trees and silent snow,
the falling snow recalling another time and frozen ponds,
skating in the dark by feel or ankling over to fetch
an errant puck, the crackle of ice in the reeds.

Step by step, he moves away from the train.
Something offers itself in the quiet. An invitation of ridges.
An odour of pitch and endlessness, of moose and bear.
But "n'ar wolf" was what he'd heard them say.

Seemed the perfect world for wolves to him.

The snow's hip deep if the crust gives way.
He used to know the way to walk like this, willing himself
to be weightless. His eyes adjust. He sees a canopy
of trees. A hillside. Ice on a rock face.

The cars call him back to their warmth and light,
little cars on a narrow track, a train to take his kids to ride,
a loop in the park. "The Bullet," they call her, watching to see
what you say, "takes her time on the grades, a train for here."

Inside, he sees Stasiuk thrashing about,
trying to sleep in his too-narrow seat. Further back,
three faces pressed against the glass wondering what he's up to,
guys in the game he'd interrupted wanting some air. He knew
the look that passed between them. *Goalies. What the hell.*
And two in the link for a smoke, eyeing the dark
creeping closer over the snow. "Jesus Ukey, what are you
doing, a guy could disappear forever out there."

Better than he deserves is what he thinks.

IV. GOALTENDER SUITE

*There must be some reason we're the only
ones facing the other way.*

– Jeff Torborg, in Thomas Boswell's
Why Time Begins on Opening Day

Rough Calculations

I lost the puck in the sun.
  – Bernie Parent

(i) *chiaroscuro*

Press one flat against your face,
even in summer, you feel its winterness.
Toss it up and down, its edges hit bone, a puck
seems leaden in the hand, a dead weight, nothing
like the subtle baseball with its endlessness,
its pendulous invitation, its pair of eights
that curl together in a perfect sphere.

Baseball. The game says grass and crackling
heat. The word allows the tongue to linger. You want
to heft a baseball in your hand, roll it across
your fingers and ponder who to let in
on its secrets, alignment of seams,
angle of elbow.
This is how you grip the sinker.
Here's the knuckleball. Le papillon.
Even those Frenchmen, mad for hockey, get dreamy
contemplating the curve and dip, the pitch's erotic path.
A baseball's hot to trot. Flat and squat, a puck's
inert, needs a lever, needs ice.

(ii) *chaotic system*

And yet, so easy to underestimate,
given its disposition to inertness, its genealogy—
your kicked rock, your frozen horse bun, pellets in a snuff tin
wrapped with tape.

Assuming the puck deforms the player's head
by half an inch, another way to know what goaltenders
know in their bones,
its weight, 6 oz., in moving from 95 mph to 0, the player's head

exerts a force over time (or impulse J) which equals
the change in momentum, Δp,

the pileup in front, crunch of blade and bone,
the puck disappears as the bodies go down, the famous
crouch, up, down, the darting eyes, looking to pick up
the shot off the stick.

Reinforcements fly over the boards, indignant
at any consideration of equals,
where, nonetheless, $F = \dfrac{\Delta MV}{\Delta t}$,

where M (the mass) and V (velocity) we know,
and Δ t, the time the puck is in contact with the player's head
and Δ t equals Δ x, the amount the head is deformed (see above)
over V, which we also know, hence F, the force—
what we want to know—equals 6060 ft. lbs.

To put it plain, what your goalie's got from the slot
is a tenth of a second.

The face a foot from the ice,
the eyes, the teeth.

(iii) *bad data point*

The '50s leap in firepower, Bernie and Bobby,
like Oppie at Alamogordo a decade before, blending the games
of boys and murder. Last man standing gets to go home
with the blonde.

The slapshot out of Montreal, born
of a desperate swipe or a Gallic snit, the style a Delacroix
or Brontë would have favoured, booming, unbridled, self-referential.
Something erotic and primal. The crowds went wild. The wings
cutting in from the boards and whaling away.

And something burning in Chicago,
the smell of trouble, sure as hell, the boys in wood shop intent
on their nail guns. Same gang. Heating up stick blades, bending them
under the dressing room door. Bobby's shot was off the glass
before you moved your head, and Dennis, Jesus,
where his was going, nobody had a clue.
"Not on your fucking life," says Tony O, in practice,
skating well clear of his goal. "Go find some other monkey.
Go see if Mrs. DeJordy raised a fool."

All this for goalies meant a whole retooling
of reflex, a new code for heart.

The crowds went wild.

One of You

Catchers in baseball, closest to cousins
in your differentness, the safeguarding home, the healing bones,
the serious gear (which ought to indicate the possibilities),
and only one of you.

Denied the leap and dash up the ice,
what goalies know is side to side, an inwardness of monk
and cell. They scrape. They sweep. Their eyes are elsewhere
as they contemplate their narrow place. Like saints, they pray for nothing,
which brings grace. Off-days, what they want is space. They sit apart
in bars. They know the length of streets in twenty cities.
But it's their saving sense of irony that further
isolates them as it saves.

Percy H. LeSueur, for one, in a fitful sleep,
flinching at rising shots in a bad light, rubbers flung
out of the crowd, insults in two languages, finally got out of bed
in a moment of bleak insight, went down and burnt a motto
onto his stick, *Haec est manus quae ictum deflecit*—
"This is the hand that turns away the blow."

Or Lorne Chabot, in 1928, when someone asked
him why he always took the trouble to shave before a game,
angled out a leg to check a strap and answered in a quiet voice,
"I stitch better when my skin is smooth."

Or dapper Charlie Rayner, who stopped a bullet
with his chin, another couple of teeth and some hasty
work to close an ugly cut. Back the next night, he takes another,
full in the face. A second night in a row, he's down, spitting
bits of tooth to the ice. "It's a wonder," he mutters,
"why somebody doesn't get hurt in this game."

Inside Jokes

The sodden weight of goal pads late in games,
30 pounds, some nights feels like 50.
No wonder horses hate the rain,
and head for shelter, steaming, under trees.
The leather soaked from sliding on the ice, the way
you get knocked about like a younger brother. The load
on shaky legs, you hope to Christ there's nothing labelled
for the corner. Weight like divers wear. Like goalies who lose
their nerve, you'd drop in a hurry and sink from sight
into an endlessness of eyes and awful teeth.

O the hell to be in Boston or, like Worsley,
in New York with boxing fans,
mushroom noses up against the glass,
the voices eerily distant, underwater insults.
Or the night an egg arcs out from the heavens to knock him
cold. Or the unforgettable weekend, back-to-back games against
Montreal and Toronto, 50 shots Saturday night, 58 Sunday.
"Dick, another debacle for the Rangers," says Danny Gallivan.
"But oh that scintillating display by the Gumper.
108 shots in two nights."

All of which he stopped but three,
losing both games.

After the second night's shelling, the others quickly
out of the showers, dressed and off to the bars downtown,
someone asks him which team gave him the worst time,
"The Rangers," says Worsley, too weary
to lift an arm to reach a smoke.

The feature that week
in his restaurant, the 'Ranger Special'—
CHICKEN SALAD SANDWICH.

Running Battle

The Montreal Forum, 1959. Toe Blake
turns away from Plante, "No goalie who plays for me
will ever wear a mask." He peels a cigarette paper out of its pack,
licks it, sticks it over his nose and, blindered, stumbles over
the sticks on the floor. "You see that? How the Christ
can you see when the puck's at your feet?"

Plante looks up at Toe from under the towel
he's pressing against his brow.

The guys steal a glance at one another. Here we go.
The first big brawl was over the toque Jacques wanted to wear
whenever he played, as if the Forum were just another frozen pond.
Toe kicked an elbow pad across the room. "You want us all
to look like fucking hicks?"

Then the running battle over the Royal York—Jacques
said the air was bad and he needed a room at another hotel.
Toe missed the garbage can again with his gum, but what could
he do? And Plante became unbeatable in Toronto, where Toe,
you know, would sell his own mother to win, and finally
we got a little peace until he woke up one day with his head
like a log and his eyes stuck shut. 5 to 1 we lose that night
and drop from first. What happened, he said to Toe,
was he that he *dreamt* about the Royal York.
Toe just stood there looking down at him,
then blinked and left the room.
You heard the latch click as he shut the door.

So here we go again, and everybody's busy
with a bit of tape or something funny about a skate.
The trainer brings Jacques a new towel, tossing the bloody one
onto the wrong pile, you wouldn't even notice until you see
Toe who's followed its looping flight to where it lands
on the whites. What's he staring at anyhow?

What makes you want to laugh is he's still
got that cigarette paper stuck to his nose.

Any Last Words (1)

Or Wilf Cude. When the name comes up
what you think of is a kind of joke: what happened the moment
he knew he'd had it with no sleep and those lunatics
waving their sticks in his face.

Pencilled in to start that night, he shakes
the ketchup bottle over his pre-game steak, pounds it
hard with the heel of his hand, miles away his mind,
what with who he had to watch that night, the war
and general state of things, the crowds falling off and teams
collapsing and all the crackpot plans to save the game.
And who's the one who gets it in the end?
The goalies. Like Charles Adams and all his firepower
in Boston insisting the League bring in an 'icing' rule.
And Art Ross wanting a puck with edges bevelled
to make it swerve and dip on its way to the net.
"Which is guaranteed to pack them in.
Defence is boring, Americans love scoring.
Look at basketball," he says.

"Be careful," says Beulah Cude, a hair
too late, and out it comes, half the bottle all over his plate.
That's when he cracks. Seems to be how it happens, something
that dumb, pushing them over the edge.

Half into his animal crouch, he gapes
at the steak where it sticks to the wall, then slowly,
dramatically, slides to the floor. Like some poor bugger
drilled by a firing squad. *Any last words and . . . oh sorry too late.*
My God. There had to be a better way to make a life, maybe
he would have that talk with his father-in-law his wife
had once and tentatively proposed.

Succinct and of his age, his epitaph to the press: "Boys,
I had to get out before they came for me
with the butterfly net."

Ulcers McCool

"How about it Frank?" says Hap Day, leaning
against the dressing room door. "There's no one else."

1945. No backups in those days, they bring down
someone out of the crowd. This was only half a joke in a country
of brash and woolly immigrants, but not in game seven,
not against Detroit.

No answer from across the room.
Hap looks at his goaltender rocking in agony,
the white leaf slowly unfolding
and crumpling.

Spring of '45, the smell of freshly-opened earth
and victory in the air and who wants to die
in the last days of a war? Halfway through game seven,
he leaves the ice. "Ulcers, what are you doing?" Hap yells—"Ulcers!
for Chrissake!!"—and hurries after him into the tunnel.

What kind of an age would name you after your affliction?
Beaky. Blinky. Cementhead. Was it callousness, or just a way
of looking something in the eye?

Again that night he'd kept Toronto
in the game. *Mother of God,* you could read
his lips as he slumped against a post when, mercifully,
the puck went up to the other end.
Safe in the dressing room now, he waits
for the milky liquid to put out the fire, slumping
under a ceiling he knows too well. That crack that looks
like a duck—how often, flat on his back, had he stared at it,
holding his breath, awaiting the sting of the needle,
the creepy tug at his brow or lip or chin?
How tired of it all he felt. He'd quack
when it was done and begin to giggle (the thought
he was crazy anyhow eased everyone's guilt a little).

Hap would always stare at him a moment then bang
on the door with his fist, "Let's go, Ulcers.
Let's go get 'em again."

The important door he leans against now,
opened only when he gives the word. He's heard
reporters working the guard on the other side. And down
the tunnel, hecklers ripping at the Wings and keeping the crowd
entertained. God how he loves it, the sticks getting up
in the crease, the whack on the ass as he sends out
his goalie again, the way his heart jumps
at the crowd's explosion.

He hears the sigh he's been waiting for
across the room, and the sound of a bottle set carefully
onto a metal table.

How about it Frankie boy? There's
no one else.

Windscape

Growing up in southern Saskatchewan, a world
as blasted and bright as a mid-winter moon,
goal was where he shone in those glittering endless games,
something in all this openness a person could manage, a zone
defined by lumps of ice pushed carefully into place.
Four foot by six. Surely this wasn't too much
to ask, order in such a small space.

Dunblane had hopes when he went up in '42,
the crops coming back, one of their own to talk about
Saturday nights in the Boston Cafe. Imagine, a boy
who learned the game on McCambridge's slough.
Maybe this was a message for everyone.
Maybe they weren't so far from the bright lights
after all. He'd have preferred a quieter city, himself,
somewhere besides New York, and fewer players with taxis
waiting as they hurried to change. What he got in the end
was a single line under his name,
brief as an epitaph:

> *Buzinski, Stephen, b. Dunblane, Sask., 1917.*
> *Games Played—9, Goals Against—55.*

Last of the class or close, and wartime too.
Then you come across the catastrophic blunder, and laugh
before you think about that windswept moment when he knew
his name would be a joke forever.
Maybe it was watching Frankie Brimsek
at the other end, that silky style he had, so effortless,
pulling down high pucks, tossing them over his opposite shoulder.
The legendary Mr Zero. You had to marvel at how smooth
he was. What in God's name did he know that made
the difference? What did he wake one morning knowing
that opened out his green and sheltered valley?

While down at his own end, a goal away
from what might have been a watershed win, Buzinski
hauls in a high shot, *Hey, looking just like Frankie,*
and tosses it over his shoulder
into his net.

The red light flashes behind the goal,
goes out as if in doubt, comes on again. The crowd
looks on in disbelief then lurches to its feet, demanding
blood. But the air goes out of the guys on the ice.
One crosses himself. One ducks what feels like something
nasty passing overhead, but it's only litter sailing through the lights.
The two teams go off the ice together, intent on changing
as fast as they decently can and getting the hell
away from the building.

Worse than taking a puck in the teeth.
Worse than finding a three-legged dog in a box
at your door.

Even Brimsek took some time to pull himself together.
Could have gone either way, they said. He looked
distinctly shaky for a game or two.

Three Little Jokes

Richard was out of the lineup that night
in 1952. A broken leg had finished Blake, but Billy Reay
was there for sure, Lach and Mosdell and Bouchard.
But I don't remember any of these. I only see
Corporal St Onge, my father's round-faced friend,
who'd got impossible tickets for the game, the first I'd seen.
At one point, I turned to see his crumpled laughing face.
Now I can't think of him any other way. He warmed in the crackle
and heat of the crowd, his eyes lit up by the heckling fan a few
rows back. The lowly Rangers had tied the game again—
Taberwit, those guys! We heard the noisy collapse
in the seat behind us, then the leap and raucous
blast—*Come on Olmstead. You turkey.*

I don't remember the outburst itself,
only the tears of bliss on Roy St Onge's face.
He'd worn his winter blues that night and had to hang on
to his wedge cap when he laughed. And when we were suddenly
on our feet, outraged as the play moved into the Montreal end
and Worsley, calmly, swung the Ranger net around
and shoved it up against the boards. Perhaps
he needed to catch his breath (the score was 4 to 4,
but the shots were more like 40 to 10). Or maybe he wanted
to needle the crowd. A rookie that year with New York, but a kid
from rugged Pointe St Charles, he stood out there, all innocence,
coolly intent on the play in the Montreal end, just as, younger,
unperturbed, he'd peer up a critical street having heard
the Frenchies were planning a foray into the Pointe.

Years later he's home, a Montreal Canadien.
He drops his bag at the door of the noisy dressing room,
glaring at ancient enemies. Nothing new to him here, fighting
to keep afloat in a chaos of fireball French. This was how
he grew up. This was like any old game tending goal
for New York. Still, in the sudden silence he feels
a little disloyal, a bit like a spy.

Amused, the players wait to take their cue
from Toe, but wonder if Worsley, tough as a stump,
might not be just what the doctor ordered. They watch him
dump his gear on the floor and shake their heads at the ratty
trapper—how well they know it and what a state it's in.
Those ragged pads. And that flimsy belly protector.
They don't know whether to laugh or cry.

As for Toe, he stares at the woeful pile a long moment, pondering
life after Plante. And what has he got himself into now?

"Where's the rest of your gear," he finally growls.

"That's all there is," growls Worsley back.

Toe sighs and nods toward the place where Plante once
changed. "Man, you must be fucking crazy."
He shakes his head and turns away.

Any Last Words (2)

There's a photograph of Wilf Cude, courtesy
of Eno's Fruit Salts, holding his goal stick in the old way,
two-handed, more like a shovel or crowbar, the Welsh face, dark,
unsmiling, a coal miner's face come into the green morning.

But this was after another kind of disaster, another
bad night in the Forum, and he was glumly home, staring
at the post-game steak he'd smothered with ketchup.
Which was how he liked it.

It took a moody night to get over a loss like that.
Then you had your knee-deep snow and pack your bag
or drag your ass to the Forum again. And he was in a strange
mood anyway, what with the sudden demise of the great Morenz,
catching an edge and crashing into the boards. Nobody even
close to him. Then Charlie Gardiner, the fiery little goalie
in Chicago, levelled at thirty after he carried his team
to an unexpected Stanley Cup. The grass
barely green as he slipped, apologizing, into a coma.
Too much for the mind of a simple man.

What touched him off was nothing—Beulah jiggled
the table (that loose leg she's asked him a dozen times to mend),
slipping the cozy off to pour his tea.

Bad timing, for sure, but she showed a goaltender's
quickness, ducking the steak that flew at the wall. He was out
the door in a morning storm, and down to the Forum
to tell them he was done.

What guaranteed his legacy was growing up
Welsh, his last words showing a heightened sense
of occasion—"By the time that steak hit the wall and stuck,
I knew I'd been a touchy goaltender long enough."
He'd looked out over the room of reporters.
"By the time it landed, I'd retired."

Big Dogs (2)

No, Terry I cannot say I ever truly understood. But Doug Harvey now, there was a horse of a different colour. I should tell this guy Doug was as good a friend as you could have. You had to love him thumbing his nose at the League because of how they got back at him for helping organize the players' union. Then he turns up in a rumpled shirt and jeans the night they finally held a night for him at the Forum. But there was another Doug Harvey night I won't forget, a near disaster in Chicago, a game against Montreal the Hawks were desperate to win. And after all the years of being doormats, the crowd was not in a generous mood. Before we even get under way, some guy at ice-level draws back his jacket just to make sure I get a good look at what he's packing. I never did mention that little detail to Helen. She was nervous about Chicago as it was. But everything went well enough until near the end, with the game close and I don't give in on a couple of dives the Hawks take, and both times, the dough-heads, while they're standing around waiting to get the call, Montreal goes up the ice and scores. The second time it got ugly fast, the crowd throwing programs and rubbers onto the ice and spitting at me through the screen. Then a couple of bottles come raining down. I retreat to centre ice and the players are getting as far from me as they can. And Clarence Campbell's at the game that night, that miserable s.o.b., he knows I'm trying to get his attention but he won't look up. The next thing you know some drunk's on the ice. "Look out!" I hear a yell, and I see it's Doug Harvey, just as this lunatic tosses a beer in my face. I grab his collar and cock my fist and it's bedlam in the building, I can tell you, and Harvey shouts in my ear, "Red, Red, you can't hit a fan. Don't hit a fan." And he pulls the guy away from me and gives me a look, then turns and smacks him in the mouth. Then seeing I'm still pissed off, he picks him up. "Don't hit a fan, Red," he shouts and slugs him to the ice again. Then there's another madman out on the ice who leaps on my back and Harvey opens his scalp with his stick. You could see a bunch of them then with one leg over the boards but they're having second thoughts when they look at these greaseballs bleeding all over the place. No doubt in my mind, he saved my neck that night. So now, for this long and happy life I have led, as I was mentioning, there's another I owe.

"All this stuff I'm telling you . . . " he hesitates for a moment and looks around the room. "Was I telling you?" He glances up, then shrugs and waves it away. "I don't know, but all this belongs to another age. The moment clearest in my mind—the moment I loved most— was when it was time to get the game under way. I'd flip the puck in the air like a coin and catch it and turn to centre ice. Oh man, you felt a charge go through the building. The crowd and both teams always kept an eye on you. The organist too—whatever he was playing, he'd stop and hit those notes that fired up everyone. My God, me too. It was magic. Especially in Montreal. In the Forum, I felt I like I was at the heart of the world. Then, this one night, just as we're getting ready to go, Terry skates out from his net to ask me a question I'll never forget."

Storey lifts his right hand and looks at it, front and back, this or that, then looks up in the fading light. "You know a few things," he says. "I hear that from what you're asking. But now I'll tell you something you don't know, because I only ever told this to one other person. It didn't make sense to me then and it doesn't now. But I'd get to thinking about it sometimes on a train alone or leaving for the Forum when I'd carefully close that door. The stained glass loose in the door there. Loose as far back as that.

"This was before the season opened sometime back in the '50s. The Wings and the Black Hawks were up north in Ontario playing an eight-game exhibition series, getting a little publicity for the League. Trouble was it was mostly bad. The Wings and Hawks didn't like each other, and every game winds up in a brawl. So the League sends me up to get things straightened out. So that's fine. I read the riot act and after the game I come back to the hotel and there's Terry and some of the Red Wings sitting around in the lobby looking bored. I always get on pretty well with the players, so I say, 'Boys, what are you doing sitting around? Why don't you get out and see a bit of the town? And someone says 'Red, it's Sunday night, nothin's open.' So I say, 'Well, I got to meet a guy, but there's a few quarts of beer in my room. Why don't you go up and help yourself and maybe I'll see you later.' By the time I get back, it's late and the boys are gone and so's the beer, big surprise. My room looks like a hurricane hit it—empty glasses and bottles on the floor, my bed messed up, cigarette butts in the sink . . . well, I don't really mind, I was like that myself when I was young. And it looks like the boys had a pretty good time so what the heck. So I don't think about it and I'm out of there early the next morning and I don't see anyone before I go. A week or two later," he says, wagging a big finger at me, "wouldn't you know it, my first game of the year is in Detroit and who's in town but the Hawks. And it's a wild one. I'm barely keeping it under control, and there's a pileup in front of the Detroit net, and you know who's on the bottom. I race in, pullin' guys off him and I say 'Terry, you all right?' And I hear this muffled voice from under the pile, 'Why don't you go fuck yourself, you drunken son of a bitch.' Hey, I'm a little shocked. A couple of guys are looking to see what I'm going to do, but I think, okay, he doesn't know who he's talking to. I always give the players a chance to cool off and what I do, I cup my hand behind my ear like this like, you know, like I didn't hear and I say, 'Terry, this is Red here, what was that you said?' And I hear him grunt as someone gives him a knee getting off, then he says, 'You didn't hear me? I said go fuck yourself you drunken *deaf* son of a bitch.'

"Hey, what choice does he leave me? 'Okay, big mouth,' I say, 'That'll get you ten. Open your yap again and you're outta here.' It wasn't my feelings were hurt. I just got mad. Here's these guys, a week or two ago, drink all my beer, mess up my room and not a word of thanks and I have to take crap like that? Any other time I would have simply clocked him. But this is where it gets into the twilight zone—I see him in Montreal a few days later, and here he's skating towards me out at centre where I'm waiting to drop the puck. Holy cow, I think, what's he going to do now? 'Red,' he says, and he looks like hell, like he hasn't been sleeping a lot, 'Red, I gotta ask you this,' he says. 'Last game there, what the heck did you give me that misconduct for?' 'What was it for, you big Palooka?' I say. 'You told me to eff off. You can't say that to a referee.' What I really wanted to say was you can't treat friends that way. He just stares at me a moment and you know how dark and scary his eyes could be, I don't even know what he was feeling, sad or sorry or angry. 'I don't remember that,' he says.

'I don't remember any of that.' And turns away without another word. Heads back to his goal. Man, you could have knocked me over with a feather, I was so discombobulated. I just stood there staring at his back as he slowly skates away. In those days, he was still wearing number one. I don't know what I was thinking. Then Henri Richard, you know, the quietest guy in the world, says, 'Red, you gonna drop that puck tonight or not? Are we gonna play hockey or stand out here looking like some idiots?'"

The Glass Door
or Any Last Words (3)

He shrugs. "Well she's the boss. Not that there's anything special I have to do," he says. "She worries I'll get too tired, that's all. That's a good one—me getting tired from talking? But, Jeez, those days . . . that was the golden age of the game for me. Something ended in 1967, the last year of the old League, the year Terry comes back from the dead. Hey just like me. Jeez. Talking about all this just takes me back. Makes me want to get back on the banquet circuit again, telling stories. That foghorn in Boston. I never did put a face to that voice. *Hey Storey! We got this town here named after you.* Just waiting for me to step out on the ice. Jeez, I even loved all that. I loved it all. Hey, I was in Corner Brook a couple of times . . . John what's-his-name . . . John Brothers, you know the guy? He's the one who'd bring me down. Never seen so much snow in my life and brother I've seen snow. I've seen everything. My life has been dangerous but terrific. That's what I say when I sign my books, see? A 'dangerous but terrific' life. And I always use three colours of ink, see? I sign 'Red' in red ink . . . yeah, kind of hokey I know. I don't get out of the house too much anymore. Close that door carefully when you go will you? I'd hate to lose it after all these years. I hope you have more luck than me trying to figure out the guy. He was a great one. Hey, one last thing I want to say before you go—be good to Doug Harvey will you? He had it rough at the end. And next time you come to Montreal we'll go have lunch somewhere. Maybe get some smoked meat. Man, how often do I think about that? Hey, maybe even go down on the Main for a steak and some french fries. And one of those fat juicy dills. God how I miss all that. Used to be a French waitress there . . . Wait a minute. Wait. Sit down, one more minute, it's okay, she won't bite, I'll tell you one last story about a goalie cracking up, Tiny Thompson, the time he blows up at his wife and fires a t-bone steak at the wall . . ."

Transition Game

Whose song this is I think I know.

Imagine the shot as a butterfly's approach.
The cat by the fence unconcerned, yet surveillant,
taking in the loop on upward air, a little dip and zigzag
there. Knowing all things converge. And where.
And wanting no truck with time.
                                    A life in the land
of do, devoid of ought and thought, which only shift the load,
the barge tilts, swings across the current, the bottom
of the Detroit river, toxic, leaden, waits.

What you watch for at the other end,
the way a changing wind flips leaves, crests become
numbers, numbers crests. The crowd's on its feet, oh yes,
what they would do, *how stupid not to do*, and five coming at me
with grim intent. I creep to the top of the crease,
begin to consider arcs and angles.
History.

This is where the cat melts into the trees.

You see the crossing pattern at the line
and sense the shifting plan, the sudden presence
at the post—*which way does he shoot?*—and brace to block
the shot or slide across and stack the pads (whose woods
these are I think I own) intent on
              where   read the turn of wrist
              and tilted blade   see it all before you see
              the hand leaps   drop to the ice to cover up   crunch
              of blades   ice   bone   mocking eyes
              familiar rasping at my ear
                    lucky lucky bohunk son of a bitch
                              shit   spit
oh sweet song live on, live on
only in my own heart sings the speed

V. CANADIAN DREAMS

Nights are worse. Darkness . . .
                                        whispers
loss is its own fur, whispers
once, once
irresistibly.

— Don McKay, "Meditation on Antique Glass"

Canadian Dreams

Halifax waterfront. Where countries of the mind
begin. The creak and sigh as a freighter rubs her ample hip
against the pier. The painted-over name says Asian heat. (A slow
canoe poles past stilted homes. Open fires. Smells of cooking chicken
in the air.) It's long past midnight here. A winter dampness cuts
to bone. Too soon to go home, we head for the one place always
open, the walls Aegean with posters of crumpled pillars. Half a dozen
tilted stools. Costas, unshaven, looks up from his chopping.
Someone broke his window last week, collapsing
an arch of golden letters. "No Turk," he shrugs.
"Just punk. I caught him by the hair."

There's one stool occupied. Cropped head in steam
above a bowl of beans, half turns, turns away.
But it's enough, the moon-face unmistakeable, not so round
now, but it's him all right. "Doug Harvey. Hey Doug." I mention
the Forum and having seen him back in 1952. He nods. His face looks
freshly stitched where someone's clipped his brow. Once he could
play the game any way you wanted, level you out in the open
or set up a play like a symphony. "So what're you doing here, Doug?
And out so late?" He hunches closer over his bowl, his voice
hoarse and tired. "Mindin' my own fucken business."

Costas wags a finger at us, European-style,
and goes back to his chopping. Our joke was to make him
wait as we bickered over the menu on the wall, then always order
fish and chips. That night we took a longer look, noticing
all the items crossed off and prices cut. And what were we up to,
ourselves, prowling the harbour at night? I thought of my father who
left the farm at seventeen to go work on the boats. He'd talk about
how they were chased by a Japanese sub, and all the whales.
But something made him quit and work on a tug. And something
made him quit the tug. Doug pays up and gives us a nod going out
that lifts our spirits again. You hate to see dreams go down
the drain. Better you take the whack on the ankle.
Something that tells you the guy's hanging on.

Porsche Turbo

Couple of beers with the boys after practice,
the kid in his purring and sleek machine. Up the ramp
and into the traffic. The lights are quick but not as quick
as him. He's ten miles out of town before he lets
it in, what happened there
out on the ice,
what weighs on him, the pass up the middle with practice
all but done, one man to beat and knowing who it had
to be—Doug Harvey, the boyhood hero,
who liked to get dressed when he wasn't hungover
or watch from the blues by himself
when he was.

And he was on the ice tonight.

"Sonofabitch. He does move good for an old guy,"
someone said earlier, wiping his bloody nose with a towel,
everybody laughing on the bench.

So here it was, too late to turn away.
Hey Hey, says one of the guys and points with his chin.
They turn at the bench to watch as Harvey glides over to gather
him in, the two of them moving up the ice together, each waiting
for the other guy to flinch. Harvey grins. The kid says later,
that's when he hears the voice in his head *you always
go to your left* and then, seeing who he is, *if you know that
he knows that.* All in a wink, you don't even think
and it's done, a tip of the cap to the left
and step to the right into open ice,
bright as a crater,
wide as a leap from a bridge.

So why the gloom as he reaches home?

He shuts down the engine and sits in the dark.
The moon lights up the Jack pine on the ridge. Another age
and he'd have been happy riding fence. Clopping along, creaking
sound in the dark, that same damn cow pushing up against the fence.
Turn in the saddle to see. Clap of thunder. Pulse of a powerful
heart beneath his own. Touch the agreeable horse
with a heel and head for home.

No one for miles around to see, he climbs out
for a leak. That moment in the dressing room he won't
forget—unwrapping an ankle, he sees the ancient skates that stop
at him. The talk in the room dies down. His eyes move up
the legs (something all wrong about them in yellow
and green), warily he glances up
at the weathered face.

"Hey," says the gravelly voice. "You always
go to your left—what the fuck were you doing out there?"

Better Days

for Don Coles

The tavern's on an ageing street. Blinking
bulbs point *here*. Inside, scattered quiet men in caps
and open coats. The walls are hung with photographs of players
from the past, Sids and Freds and Charlies. What you notice
in the photos is their gear—everything's too tight or small,
except the grins and tumbling hair. It's a different age.
They look a little sheepish playing games.

The home team's on behind the bar, the sound
turned low. Nobody's paying much attention.
Someone down the bar says, "A woman can do that
to you." Someone adds, "In the wink of an eye." I see the heads
bob sadly in the glass, then hear a half-known voice at my ear,
"You're watchin' the hockey. You know me, Doug Harvey.
Bet you wouldn't turn a thirsty guy away."
When had I thought of him last, I wondered,
surprised at what gets left behind. I nod to the woman,
who shrugs and moves her cigarettes away. She knows him
too, but for her he's just a bum who's cadged a drink.
He gives me a bat with his hand, "Hey, what about one
for my friend while you're at it?" I see there's
a move or two he can still put on you.

I look at the hand as it rests by my arm
and think of what it's known, the backs it's slapped
in better days, a drunken fan it flattened twice to save a referee.
Then that seventh game in overtime, fooled by Leswick's
floater—he reaches upward, almost tenderly,
as if to touch a shyly offered breast, tipping the shot
past a startled McNeil. I watch as he turns in the mirror
and moves between the chairs and brooding figures
back to his table by the wall. My knowing how
he moves is exact and ancient. He reaches home,
a drink in each hand. I see him turn to find me in the glass.

"Hey, the joke's on you, I got no friend."

120

No Time to Go

The last guys, White and me, slow to get out
of our gear—him on his way up, savouring a solid game,
me, another cigarette. Old friends, the after-game aches
and smokes. Hurts just to get a decent drag, my ribs
again where I land on someone's skate.
Red's gone, his last words being, "What do you say
we get Rutledge into a game or two?" Hey, no argument
from me. There's a change from the old days in Detroit he must
be thinking. Outside, the heat and stinking air, the traffic,
even on a Sunday afternoon, ramps and madmen.
How did Larry Regan talk me into this?
Sunny California, he says to me.
Bring out the family. Live on the Beach.

Shitty ice. Shitty crowd again this afternoon, biding
their time from brawl to brawl. Tossing litter onto the ice
to keep themselves amused. Kelly says, taking me
out of the game, "Ukey, I'm not blaming you,
half these guys are walking in their sleep."
I lob a wet sock at the wall. White says, "Tropical hockey.
They must be mad." He says, "After a game, you want to walk out
into snow, Chicago, Toronto, anywhere coconuts don't grow.
Maybe Chicago." And tells me one about Billy Reay.

"The Hawks down 6 to 1 with seconds to go, the guys they
had then, man, and out of the playoffs early again, and he sends
out this kid with Mikita and Hull, says to him you take the faceoff.
Mikita and Hull, who hardly ever play together, why now, and the
kid's a defenceman, hasn't been out on the ice in a month. Who
knows what Billy's thinking, nobody's looking too hard to see.
Maybe it's see you later for somebody, maybe he's telling the kid
he should think about something over the summer—maybe Billy
doesn't forget when he wants him quick in Boston once and the kid's
so bored he's down the bench with his skates undone. *You take the
faceoff.* So here they are five goals down and no time to go,
he takes a long and hard look at the clock and Mikita

on one side and Hull on the other, then skates
back to the bench and says, "Billy
you want me to win this?
Or just tie it up?"

That's how he ends up out here in fantasy land
playing for Mister Finley and wearing
white skates.

Prairie boys wearing white skates.

There's guys getting hold of this game
been out in the sun too long.

Out of the Sun

Piano bar after an ugly game (bad scene
at the buzzer). None of the boys from either team
around, we meet for a couple of brews. Blonde in a shimmery
dress at the bar fending off two assholes. Black guy playing some
blues in a corner. Built like Leo Boivin, not much bench
unoccupied. "Smooth," says the kid, "Fats Domino,
Chubby Checker—you ever make the connection, Bill?"

Reminds me how he says to me once, "Enola Gay.
It's backwards, Bill, it's code—You Are Going Alone.
Jesus. Alone for the rest of your life. We think
we get jerked around." Still spending a lot of
time alone yourself, I say. "Not enough,"
he says and grins. I ask about the trade and how he likes it
out in California. "Yeah, it's great. Wouldn't have missed it
for the world. California." And mentions a night against Montreal,
Meloche can't keep us in the game all by himself. He's taken
so many shots he can't bend over to loosen his pads and
Glover goes up one side of him and down the other.
Another time Finley himself breaks into a game
to announce all Golden Seal tickets on sale for half price.
You have to laugh, I say. "You do," he agrees.
"But where's it going, this fucking game?"

However you cut it, it's crappy getting traded.
Always comes out of the sun. *Sorry to say you don't fit
into the plans any more.* I ask how he liked it in Chicago,
playing for Tommy Ivan and Billy Reay. Oh, they taught him
a lot, gave him a lot to think about. Like what? I ask.
"Like never trust two guys with four first names," he says.
"Lessons everywhere," he says and tosses a twenty on the table.
"Always a pleasure, Bill. Give my regards to the boys."
He watches the piano player a moment, watches his fingers
melting over the keys. I see the blonde holding his eye
in the mirror. The assholes turn to give him a look,
then sink a little lower on their stools.

Our Trio

Homer's heroes were certainly no braver
than our trio, but more fortunate: Hector
was excused the insult of having
his valour covered by television.
                    – W. H. Auden, "Moon Landing"

Someone wanted a bench out on the 'battleground'
for authenticity. So our three huddle together
looking ill at ease. They don't like the feel of an arse
on a bench at the best of times, but what they fear most is looking
like fools. Instinctively, they don't much like these guys or what
they're up to here, but the word has come down from on high.
One stares longingly at the team gliding by.
One studies the blade of his stick, smoothing an end
of tape. What can you say in battle gear that doesn't sound
fatuous? Sadly, they sense this. Think of grimy Hector,
working his gum to ease his nerves, asked to look at the monitor
and comment on his deeds that day. Or the Greeks, miked up
in the humid horse, arguing over what they'll say
for the camera, descending the ladder.

"So what's the game plan boys?" the interviewer asks
to get things rolling. "What were those golden thoughts when
you woke this morning?" The boys do all they can. "We win each battle
on the boards, we'll be okay." "Howie, this team does its talking
on the ice." While not a week before in a different city,
our three concoct a brilliant goal in overtime,
a coughed-up puck, two letter-perfect
passes and a tip-in off the post.

You see their relief when someone signals *wind it up*.
"Before you go though, boys, how about a big thumbs up for the fans
at home?" Heart-rending how hard they work to oblige, to ensure
a proper manner for a proper audience who, if they existed,
would have been decent enough to be doing
something else when this was on.

Guys like Pete Goegan

We still went under the system, then, that praise
to the face was open disgrace.
          — Hemingway, *A Moveable Feast*

Guys like Pete Goegan, sent out by Adams
to settle a score or get something going, throwbacks
to Jack's own day when, bleeding, you'd swing by the bench
for a swipe with a sponge, the clouding bucket an emblem of pride
in a simpler time, players with slicked-down hair
hurrying back and forth along the boards.

Pete Goegan. His name would come up
years later, mentioned by Walt McKechnie on the bus,
the Golden Seals on a terrible slide, another collapse at the end,
the seats in the dark slowly filling, guys bandaged and beat
and deflated, but shifting over to share a seat, careful
not to mention the good move or save or giving up the body
for the team. The voices down in the back are subdued, the talk
of a nose rearranged, a glove flapped in the face of a disliked
opponent. You hear the quiet approving laughter, the talk
down the old road, old debts erased, the scraps and skirmishes,
pastings of mythological proportion, toughest of the tough—
the blood in the bucket still at the game's true heart.
The smaller guys, the skill guys and skaters
like Gilbertson, who took a bad whack in the corner
tonight, listen mainly, knowing their place
at the edge of things.

McKechnie, the veteran, stretches back
like an old scarred cat. You sense a hint of weariness
in a world so familiar, the gloom of a mid-season slump,
his place on the bus and its heat on his ancient legs,
a loosened tooth he tests with the tip of his tongue,
the last word left for him. "No contest," he says,
the meanest son of a bitch he's ever seen
was Pete Goegan. "He'd put out your eye as soon
as shake your hand. He'd pitchfork his mother."

Nodding, we stare out the windows, watching stragglers
leaving the Stadium. One points out the idling, darkened bus
with a shout and hurls himself against the chain-link fence.
Half watching, some of the older guys mull over
how you end up in the life you do.
The younger ones, which side of the ice
Goegan played and how they might measure up.
And maybe where was the guy or two
they knew who'd lost an eye.

And then, intruding into the silence,
an unexpected voice—Gilbertson, his words
as soft and perfectly timed as one of his passes,

"Put out your eye," he says.
"The son of a bitch. You know he'd only do that
to me twice."

VI. SAINTS AT HOME, SOLDIERS BETWEEN WARS

They flee from me that sometime did me seek
With naked foot stalking in my chamber.

– Thomas Wyatt

Ascension

"Oh he could be a son of a bitch," says Ted,
who ought to know, Ted Lindsay, the captain, leader
at the infamous Battle of the Soo, first man into any fray,
forget it's an exhibition game. For six full minutes slugs it out
with Red-Eye Hay. They catch their breath and start again
in the penalty box, finally going at it in the stands with cops.

Or, fiercely, toe to toe with Ezinicki of the Leafs,
Lindsay, five-foot-eight and giving 20 pounds away, nonetheless,
knocks him cold. They shift him onto the metal table, where slowly
Wild Bill wakes and, in a silver drifting moment, contemplates
his worldly line of work—eleven stitches from his hairline
to his brow, four in his mouth where Lindsay broke a tooth,
four more up the side of his head. While Terrible Ted
needs one, a single stitch in a hand so swollen
he can't make a fist for a week.

"Yes, toss a cup of rice at Terry and he'd catch it all,"
says Ted. "But he could be one son of a bitch,
and kept the other guys on edge."

Even in photographs over the years when they won,
the guys hastily gathered, grinning and half undressed, dripping
champagne, you see his gradual ascension, his drifting up
toward the top, far from where you want your goalie,
front and centre, rumpled and content.
In 1961, after they take out Toronto, everyone
around him seems to turn away. You see his hands rest
heavily on Howe's and Ullman's shoulder pads, but Gordie
ooo's the other way with Sid, and Normie leans toward the lens.
The two beside him turn away, re-rumpling happy team-mates'
hair. Bemused, the guy behind leans further back as if to cock an ear
at noises in the vent above his head. Left to himself, Terry's
dreamy, miles away, his mind perhaps on how to scale
that wall, as captured heroes do, and pry
the grating off and get away.

Game Days

Woke to an unwelcome darkness at the window,
the clock unset, no singsong call through the locked door,
the silence out there too familiar. What woke me?—those kittens
she got to get rid of mice off the golf course. Nervy buggers,
cats, they gallop over the bed. Who let them in?
The door locked, as I said.

Slept on my bad side again, the elbow slowly
disintegrates. More bone for the jar when the season's
done. Slowly, I come to the surface and there they are. Locked
in a fierce embrace, they rip at each other and bump together
over the floor. One disengages, distracted by a toppled
shoe. The other creeps closer, tail twitching,
ready to leap, that moving-not-moving cat's trick with motion.
I think of Backstrom—Lucky I call him, he can't figure
why. He glances up and his stick comes off the ice.
Hey Lucky, how do you feel tonight?
God there's moments you love the game.

There's the phone, Lefty having a heart attack.
Quickly I dress and come into the kitchen's gaping silence.
There's where my plate hit the wall. Goaltender's theatre.
A woman and children taken to the road like refugees.
I close my eyes and hear an unrepentant murmur
from the living room, some dreary talk show
guest—"I'm not your girl next door,
if you want to know."

The sound left low as always game days.

I see the bedroom game is done.
They sit like glass cats on the bottom step,
turning their heads together, watching as I leave.
Their eyes peer out at me from a world of well-timed leaps
and near catastrophes, unexplained absences,
the skill that makes them cruel.

How Things Look in a Losing Streak

(i)

That voice as we leave the ice, "Go home ya bums.
Get a shower ya need one." We looked at the one fat guy
still up in the gallery. "Who gets to kill him?"
someone behind me muttered.

The greaseball on TV over the bar, so pleased
with his wit and his marvellous chin, "Folks, this has gotta be
the day's big surprise, those Detroit Dead Things
lose again."

Then the little weasel from the morning paper,
"The Wings blow another one, fans, but Terrible Terry
seems more himself, cursing yours truly and heaving a skate
at our head. Hey, maybe things are looking up."

Gadsby came over after the game from a table
of Rangers. I noticed the others lean their heads together,
and one, a new kid who'd picked up a couple under his eye,
glanced over, grinning. "Sitting by yourself, Terry?"
said Gadsby. "That's quite a lip you got there."
Whose face is worse, I said to myself,
looking at his battered nose.
The talk as always, who's up, who's down,
how do you know when to go, nobody's got a clue.
"Ukey," he leans down and looks me straight in the eye.
"You know I never said what they said in the *Times*.
Tweet Tweet? Jesus Christ.
Would I make fun of a friend like that?"

His look the same as he gives me late in the game,
trying to pull me over against the post.

(ii)

Another short night by the time I get home.
I toss and turn for a couple of hours then come out
behind the house to try to sleep. The morning sun feels good
on my bones and I'm watching the one bee in the garden's
tough last flowers, when around the house she comes
waltzing, golden brown from the sun, saying how do you do,
she only just moved in and heard that a hockey player
lived down the street. Well, here I am, not a stitch on
and my lower lip puffed up from last night. I shift
the newspaper over myself and we talk from a suitable
distance—how warm for late in the year, how dull it is here
after living downtown, her husband who leaves in the dark
and comes home in the dark. I find myself watching that bee
as he labours from flower to flower, his legs and back end
hanging down, how aerodynamic can that be?
Awkwardly, he hauls himself into the coarse yellow
petals and struggles toward the sweet centre. Stopped,
he untangles himself and tries another way,
flipping his wings in frustration, and I'm pulling
for him though you'd think by now, the end of October,
he'd have this down better.

When I turn to look she's gone, the blades of grass
unbending where she walked away.

That's when it hits me my own days
are numbered. Long after she's gone, I glance
at the paper still flat on my lap with all its freight
of another day's unfolding.
A breeze flips a page and, Jesus,
wouldn't you know, there's Gadsby's ugly face
grinning up at me.

Et toi, Marcel?
or **Solitude**

It would have killed him once, the battle
with his mother in the afternoon. Grocery money,
that's where it started. But then she got onto his moods
and his drinking again and how everyone dreaded
the sound of his glass on a TV tray
in the morning.
What he saw now in her fury
was himself. And what could he do but laugh
when he heard how she got herself to the game on her own
that night, and sat up in the Chicago section. She spoke
to no one, gave no sign of any affiliation. All night
long she listened as they jeered at her son and called him
names. "Hey that's what we pay our money for," someone
howled, slapped a friend and sat back loudly on his plastic chair.
A part of her was outraged but another whispered,
Jump right in and join the fun.

It takes a load off, knowing
everybody lets you down in the end.
And nobody knows this better than goalies.
That's why they want to get off
on their own.

There's a photograph of Gadsby as a Red Wing
glancing back at his famous deflection.
It's not the puck his eyes are on, but Terry's
lifted pad. Gadsby's hope is one last bailout. Helplessly,
the goalie's bullet head turns back to the space his body has just
vacated. You sense a huge abandonment here, an end of something
more than just a season. The moment seems one of uncommon
cruelty, a fluke from beginning to end, Baun's floater
from the point, a redirect off your own defenceman,
a puck that barely falls over the line.
This was Terry's final moment with Detroit,
the second time they traded him away.

Even Pronovost, as good a friend as a goalie had,
a rock in front, a cannon bolted into concrete on a cliff,
put three past Sawchuk in a single game. One off his elbow,
one off his skate and—what a nightmare—a third
he meant to get rid of behind the net. All he wanted
after the game was off the ice and out of the rink.
But he knew, before he left the dressing room,
he needed a word with his goalie.

"'Forget it, Marcel,' he tells me,
pulling his chest protector over his head, that useless
piece of gear he wears as long as I know him, the leather
all mildew, the padding flattened long ago. Oh Jesus,
what went through my mind, I wanted to jerk it
over his head and stomp it and rip it to pieces—
I guess I was wanting him to shout at me
or something. You never had a clue with him.
You never knew what the fuck to expect.

'Forget it, Marcel,' he tells me
and takes a long drag on his cigarette. 'At least
you beat me clean on all three.'"

Things in Our Day

"He had rabbit ears—you watched what you said before a game."
As Gary Bergman speaks, his eyes take in the tables in the gloom. Old
defenceman's eyes. "Some days he didn't care, but you never knew.
And then that dreadful stuff he rubbed all over himself before he put
on his gear—Red something . . . Red Man . . . Red Devil . . . the stink
of it, my God. What with that and the short fuse, the guys gave him
and his gear a wide berth. And I wore number two, you understand?
That was my number all the way up through minor hockey, but I never
gave any thought to where it might land me one day. I get to Detroit
and it hits me, jeez, I'm dressing next to a legend. The guys were
always bitching about that liniment, but I never opened my mouth. By
the time I'd get my gear on, though, my eyes would be tearing so bad
I'd have to grope my way toward the door. Oh man. He was a great
one. But getting dressed next to him was no picnic."

All the while, I see he's carefully weighing the quiet that seems to have
settled around us. There's not another white face in the bar. And his is
as wide and bright as a harvest moon—much fuller than when I watched
him play—and pale, and he's shaved his head. That surprised me when
he pulled up to the curb, sunglasses and shaved head, though even in his
playing days his hair was fair and always pretty sparse. Nobody knows
him now, he says. Who remembers a stay-at-home defenceman with no
hair? He laughs and tells me that's been his salvation. It's given him a lot
of freedom with his family. "Half of Terry's surliness was only wanting
to be left alone," he says. "He didn't like the limelight, fans all over you,
wanting to sit at your table and tell you how great you were. He knew
how quick they turned when things weren't going so good." Bergman
signals a waiter, who seems in no hurry to come to our table. He's
talking to me but he's keeping one eye on the waiter. "Ukey would give
it right back to them too. Boston was always the place we hated to play.
Some of those fans, man, they'd take the hide right off you. To get to
the ice, you had to go down this little strip of linoleum and you knew
what was waiting at the other end. And Terry had his history there in
Boston . . . They'd be on him even before the game began. One time he
goes after someone, straight over the screen in his gear. We all converge
on this big mouth about the same time, Ukey, the cops, the rest of the

guys. What a scramble in the seats, people trying to get out of the way. One of the cops gets a shoe slashed open." He gives a little shake of his head, remembering. "Everybody grabbing at everybody."

The waiter brings menus and stands there waiting. We order and he leaves without a word. Bergman watches him go then leans toward me. "What are you doing in this part of town anyway," he asks. The university, I say. The Detroit papers on microfilm. Microfiche. He looks at me. "Microfeesh. What the hell is that? You think you'll find out about him from the newspapers? He hated those guys." He's quiet a moment, looking at me as if he's assessing how much of a dunce he's talking to here. Sips at his water then sets the glass down. "You happen to notice nobody parks at a meter down here? You think that's just coincidence?" Casually the waiter slides our plates onto the table, pours coffee and asks if there's anything else we want. No *have a good day* from this guy. Bergman lifts a corner of the bread and says more sauce would be nice. The waiter shrugs and brings him a bottle. Bergman coaxes a little out and looks at me, "You want a Sawchuk story? Put that pen down. I'll give you a Sawchuk story, but you gotta look at me."

He sets the sauce bottle out of the way, then moves a vase with plastic weeds from the centre of the table. "Things in our day were different, you understand? You go to a hockey game now and what do you get? Basketball music. Goalies? Jeez, what do they look like?—guys from the bomb squad. Something else, we always played an exhibition game against the farm team during the season. You know, bring in the big team for the local fans. You never knew when. So in '62 or '63, we're going pretty good, we're in the hunt and having fun and Terry and Gordie are playing like their old selves. This one Saturday night . . . hey, you want to know how good those guys really were?" he interrupts himself. "One night before a really big game, a game we absolutely have to have, I'm getting dressed next to Terry and I don't know how *he's* feeling, but I'm a wreck, and Gordie stops and asks him how he's doing. 'Pretty good, big guy,' Terry says. 'Just get me a couple and we should be okay.' Well, it was a battle that night but we come out on top and what do you think?—we win the game two to one. Gordie gets both goals and Terry knocks down everything but something he had no chance on at the end. When those two got it going, man, I'm telling you . . . but that little chat they had before the game?—whenever I think about it, I get the willies."

"Anyway," he looks at me a moment as if it was me who interrupted him. "Anyway, this other night we've got a big game up in Toronto, huge game, Saturday night, Hockey Night in Canada, the whole show, and they tell us we have to play another game the night before in Hamilton. Hamilton Red Wings, our Junior team. And Ukey's pencilled in for both games. Back-to-back games they want him to play, so the fans in Hamilton get to see him, and here we are battling for a playoff spot. Does that make sense? 'Terry,' they say, 'it'll give you a little extra playing time.' He's in the League then thirteen, fourteen years. 'Playing time,' he says, 'What the hell do I want with playing time?'"

Bergman picks up his water glass again and looks into it closely as if he'd seen something floating in it. "So you know he's not too happy taking warm-up shots that night. Waving at pucks." He shakes the glass and then puts it down without taking a drink. He shakes his head. "He was a terrible practice goalie anyhow. Anyone will tell you that. Wanted to save himself for the games, he'd say. The guy plays twenty years in goal—nobody else had lasted more than eleven before him. So maybe he wasn't so crazy. Anyhow we knew enough to keep the puck down. Most of us were scared to death of him anyway. So here's these pumped up kids bouncing up and down at the other end and stealing looks at us and we're trying to work up a little interest and lobbing fat ones into his trapper or whacking them ten feet wide off the boards. Or off the bricks. That building—whoever put it up didn't know much about hockey, that was easy to see. The boards were too high and flush against the pillars. Man, some hare-brained kid runs you from behind, how easy would it be to lose your head? The walls at each end are brick, too, and tight against the boards. And over Terry's head there's the biggest portrait of the Queen you've ever seen, painted right onto the brick, fifteen feet by twenty, easy. *Ice* hockey, I remember thinking, that's what she would have called it, right? You call it ice hockey, what do you know about the game? Am I right? Still, I'm looking into that steely gaze and thinking whatever she had going on in her head, you'd never know it looking at her eyes. Anyways, the guys are bored and someone flips a puck at her nose, and

I get to thinking what have *we* got to bitch about? Imagine being *her* with all those royal jerks around her and scandals and scumbag writers. Talk about no place to hide. And just then the ice goes dark and the lights go up on her for the anthem. It happens all of a sudden and Ukey turns around quickly, wanting this all over with. And one of the boys had just ripped a long one toward the net and the puck sails through the dark and smacks Terry right behind the knee there where he's got no padding. Oh Lord, I'm thinking, here we go. All you can see against that lit-up wall is Terry's silhouette. He just goes rigid like someone shot him from the stands, then sort of slithers down the goalpost to the ice. My mind is racing. I don't even think about him being hurt and so much at stake for the team. All I can think, he's going to kill someone. One of his own guys, right in front of all these people. Right in the middle of the national anthem. And then, don't ask me how it happens, I start to giggle. It's just terror, like when you're kids and you're laughing at the table and you know your old man's just about to blow his top, but you're helpless, man, you can't stop? Right? And then I sense these darker shadows all around me—the guys are doubled over holding onto one another. Then you see that silhouette of Terry slowly hauling himself up the post and flopping over the crossbar. Man, the guys just lose it, it's terrible but no one can help it. I see them in that weird light holding onto each other, collapsing on the ice together. Hysterical that's what we were. And the eeriest thing about it was it's all in complete silence, except for the crowd droning on, you know, *send her victorious happy and glorious.*"

He stops and looks at me. "Jesus. Who writes crap like that? Tell me you don't write crap like that." He catches me by surprise and I have to stop myself from laughing. Then I think about your nerves before a game—guys rocking from skate to skate during the anthem—all you want is to get things going, and every night that awful droning on and on. And I get a sudden rush of how much I'm enjoying Bergman and this place and our waiter, who's looking at us now, maybe a little amused, and everyone else is ignoring us altogether. Some tentative seal of approval maybe. So I say, "I don't write stuff like that, Gary. Swear to God. And if I ever did, I'll never do it again." He stares at me and shakes his head. "Man," he says, "that's embarrassing—even I know that."

He picks at his french fries, which are cold by now, then looks at me. "So anyway—hey, I told you put that pen down—anyway, there we are and the anthem's getting near the end, and the guys are trying to get back on their feet before the lights come on. You hear this buzz in the crowd, they know something's going on. It's a nightmare, I'm telling you. And nobody's going to go near the goal to wish him luck. We're holding our breath, waiting to see what he'll do." Bergman sits back from the table and gives this little chuckle. "You know what he does? He doesn't even look at us. Straight off the ice he goes, up the tunnel and into the dressing room. Doesn't say a word to anyone. The coach. Trainer. Doesn't even slow down at the bench. Someone said, 'I bet he was into his third gin and tonic before the first period ended.' Someone else said, 'Yeah, he was moving pretty good for a guy with a bad leg.'"

Bergman's quiet for a moment, looking at the water glass he's holding in both his hands. "Yeah, you never knew. He could be a dark and scary guy, but you never knew. Took a lot of shots in his time. Sometimes, though, when things got really hot and heavy, we're hanging on for our lives or trying to kill a penalty in a game we need, and here comes their big line over the boards, that's when you'd see his eyes get really bright behind his mask. Delight and panic at the same time, maybe . . . who could say? But that's when he was most alive. Out on the ice with the game on the line. Even with all it cost him in the end. That's what I think anyway."

Leaving the bar, we nod to the waiter, who turned out to be pretty friendly. Bergman pays an armed attendant at the parking lot and climbs into his car. "Microfeesh," he mutters. "What next?" He looks up at me a moment, then offers his hand out the window. "You know," he says, "before I came up, I had a year or two of university myself. In our day, you kept that kind of thing to yourself."

What I Liked About Bars

Was the neon invitation, the glow
down the block on a bad night, a tramp's
hieroglyphic on a likely gate, was the taxi burbling off,
was the way you stamped off snow in the doorway,
careful not to give the wrong impression,
was what the place gave out of someone's dream,
the photographs, the antlers gathering dust, a ship's barometer
you tapped for luck, was the clatter of caps and slam of cooler doors,
was the little notes the girls stuck up for each other by the phone
and the way they had with regulars, the teasing interrupted
talk, was knowing they'd always be back to their ashtray
under the bar, was knowing the route exactly
to the can, was the mirror's doubled bottles, those that ended up
in the back, Aquavit and Metaxa, Galliano, long-necked
and lethal, the bartender's best friend.

What I liked about bars was the way they shoe-horned
you into the night. Someone you've seen before sends over
a drink. *Tough night, Terry.* Somewhere not far, a woman's low
distracted laugh. You hear her murmur something, excusing
herself. You wait to hear her voice behind you,
or see her purse as it sags on the bar by your arm.

What I liked was no one pressed you
to look at a tap or take a troubled daughter back
to bed. You couldn't just go home, your head still rattling over
the one you made at the end or didn't. Or something some bastard
said from their bench. Bloody Pilote, the way he gets under
your skin. How could you think about riddles and hens
and trains that could when you knew you couldn't.
Some nights it hurt just to breathe.
Then you had your assholes in the greys.

So here I am again, looking down
into an unfamiliar street. Some things don't change,
this radiator's welcome heat, or how the snow begins,

that sparse and aimless swirling past the lights.
And there's the purse again, collapsed on the floor
like a daughter's indispensable animal
tumbled off the bed.

"Are you leaving so soon?" I hear her murmur
into her pillows. A draft from an ill-fitting window
stirs a mobile over her bed. "Has it started
snowing yet?" she asks.

But she won't wake up enough to hear,
even if I answer.

Time After Time

A stillness of monastic cells. Films and boxes
in disarray. I close my tired eyes a moment under the cowl.
The film whistles over the spools. I think how painters use mirrors
to look at their work and proofreaders like to read lines
in reverse. But what am I looking for here?
You notice the camera can't leave him alone. The clock
momentarily stopped, you see his restless moving from post
to post, the desultory sweeping in his crease. All he can manage.
I think of Bower's confusion one season when Terry brings back
a station wagon Johnny fixed up with a car dealer friend,
mud-spattered (where in hell had he *been* with it?), shambles
of bottles, hair bands, cigarette packs. "He's your friend,"
says Armstrong, not easy to know himself.
"You figure him out."

I start with the faceoff again, unravel the travel of eyes,
the mask moving up to the clock, then over the opposition bench,
who's on, who's off. Time after time he shuts them down,
the shots kicked aside or rocketed into the glass.
Flat on the ice, he hooks the puck to safety with his stick.
Slowly the opposition gets off him. Legend or not,
he gets the knee like anyone else, the son of a bitch,
the way he cuts the heart right out of you.

Closing time in the archives too, time for one last look.
The sun slipping under the leaves at the second floor window.
A glimpse of the sluggish Ottawa below. Eddy's Matches
used to be over there somewhere. Gone now, how long?

Jesus how did he see he did how
JESUS, the puck nipping out of his trapper
back to their sticks, the clever pass play unravels,
all the way into their end and the critical faceoff, the puck
jumping into the straightening referee's hand. Then hopping back
onto the boards without a glance, they plump down neatly
between their grimacing team-mates.
Somebody else go give him a whirl, Jumping Jesus.

VII. HURT HAWKS

No more to use the sky forever but live with famine
And pain a few days: cat nor coyote
Will shorten the week of waiting for death, there is game
   without talons.

– Robinson Jeffers, "Hurt Hawks"

An Ancient Fire

It's a terrible photograph of Terry, blurry,
doctored in an amateurish way. Still,
in the deep slump of his body you see his agony
and sagging spirit. It's a close place. Chicago, 1967,
last go-around for an ageing team, last of the Six Team League.
When he goes down, you get your waltzing in the crease,
some half-hearted shoving, a tepid insult or two,
but everyone out there knows the name of the game.

He was flat on his face for fifteen minutes.
He'd only just come into the game when Hull
wound up and let one go. It looks at first as if his head
is gone. You take a closer look at the photograph and try
to sort out what belongs to whom, and you see he's on his feet
but he's turned his back on his crease and the milling players
and Haggart, the trainer. And who could blame him?
Baun looks worried but keeps his distance.
Haggart comes closer but warily.
You look at Terry's lowered head and wonder
at the crudely touched-up curly hair (where does *that*
come from?). You think of beaten soldiers slogging back
to the beach. Twenty years of taking heavy shots,
of having to rally your nerves, now this
howdy doody Ukey blast from Hull.

The signs of defeat are clearly there. The taped-up
hand that holds the damaged arm. The body that only
wants to curl into itself. The terminating 30s on his sleeves.
You know there's not a lot of chatter on the bench.
Imlach's got his hat tipped back in misery,
a second goalie down. It's a close place,
the score tied at two, the series at two,
a season and more that dangles by a thread.
It may be a bad photograph, but it caught
a weighty moment in the age.

The crowd's on its feet and the singing begins.
Some are amazed that he ever got up, but they all join in.
Good Bye, Terry, Good Bye, arm in arm they sway from side
to side, the singing rising, soaring,
lifting the building.

Wouldn't you know it, though, he snarls
when Haggart asks him how he feels—"*I stopped
the fucking puck didn't I?*"—and turns to glare in his fury
at—who? Pilote? Not Hull? What's up here?
What's this about? Haggie's craning,
trying to see and feels the creep of hair up the back
of his neck. Something's happening here. Precariously,
he turns and slips and skids toward their bench.
He's got to get back to Punch with the news.
He won't even wait for a helping hand.

The Thousand Things

"You better stay down, Terry."
Pilote cuts lazily through the crease, speaking
to the crumpled goalie at his feet.

Sawchuk was down, face flat on the anaesthetic ice.
So here was the luxury of disaster, the dreamy letting go
the thousand things. Let someone else look after
everything now. Slide and glide for him.
He knew exactly what was on the way when Hull got room
to let one fly. His choices were few: come out and cut down the angle
or go take that job with his father-in-law. A hundred and twenty
miles an hour, he takes one full force on his shoulder.
The crack of bone like a roof beam giving way.
He hears familiar voices kneeling close. "Man, oh man.
He hits the ice like he's been shot." "Those useless goddamn
shoulder pads, how many times do I tell him that?"

He hears the mocking serenade begin again.
What does he care about the crowd? He's heard it all before.
In this world, though, the softly spoken words are the hardest
to swallow. *You better stay down, Terry.* And Terry hears
his own guys at the net. "You hear that little prick?"
"And skating through the crease like that." Stemkowski
says nothing, watching Pilote skate slowly back to his bench.

So, Pilote was the one who fanned the flame.
By the time he stepped off the ice, he was having second
thoughts himself. You'd have said Terry was done the way
he went down. But you don't need to look around now
to know who's on his feet. The singing fades away.
Billy's peering at him down the bench, tapping
his head beneath his hat—"Wake the fuck up."
Pilote takes a swig of water and spits it out.
Jesus. Jesus. Jesus. And hadn't he felt those eyes
on him all the way back to the bench. Bloody Stemkowski.
The corners were going to get interesting too.

Something Burning in Chicago

They came in waves then, Hull and Mikita, Maki and Mohns
with a heavy shot of his own, hulking Esposito, speedy Wharram,
then Hull again. Billy Reay back and forth behind Chicago's bench,
jabbing a guy in the back to go. But he couldn't take his eyes off
Sawchuk's mask, the way it swung deliberately from side
to side. What did it remind him of?—something seen

in a dream or on TV. What was going on behind the mask?
How could you know? The injured arm seemed fine.
The self-absorbed sweeping after he'd slowly pushed himself
to his feet, the lazy arc of blade from post to post, Billy hadn't seen
that in a while. It made him uneasy. The heavy traffic didn't seem
to faze Terry either, Hull flailing with his elbow at the mask.

Again and again, the Hawks came on like a storm at sea
on a sightless night, the only hope was feel what was coming
and face it straight-on. 37 shots he blocks in the 40 minutes he plays
after Bower goes down, the wildest time when Stemkowski goes
for tripping at 4:23 and then again at 10:13 in the third,
and Punch explodes, his hat half knocked off, climbing up

over his players to curse the referee for a homer. Stemkowski,
who'd put the Leafs ahead by one and watched and waited and caught
Pilote in a corner, pounding him senseless, Stemmer, the only one
who'd dare to imitate Sawchuk's shambling gait, dragging
his knuckles over the dressing room floor. Ukrainian too, born,
like Terry, in Winnipeg, the one team-mate Sawchuk sought out.

"Why don't you stay downtown," he'd say. "We'll go for a beer
at the Isabel after the game. Bring in your shaving kit." The last guy
Terry would leave dangling out on a limb. Five on four, the Hawks
set up their points, moving the puck from corner to corner, looking
to find the open man. Four minutes short-handed—it seemed
like forever. One shot after another Terry took to the body,

letting the puck land safely at his feet, then dropping

to cover it up. Nervously the home crowd eyed the clock.
The hats dipped in bitter disappointment, then turned to one another
for assurance. The Hawks were a scoring machine but how many times
had they let the big ones get away. All game, Hull had been shooting
up around Sawchuk's head, wanting him back on his heels and deep

in his crease. Bobby thought it was funny, giving people
a whack with the puck. In practice, just for a joke, he'd bounce
a shot off the seats near the women sweeping out the aisles.
But this was different, this was a battle over the angles,
a deadly geometry—one or two degrees would make the difference.
A goal was all Chicago needed to tie the game and open the gates.

This time Hull drops a shoulder, feinting high but ripping one
low for the post, hoping to catch him rising up. But Terry
gambles on his eyes and brain. He hasn't forgotten how Hull
made him look so bad in game two. This time he holds the deep
crouch and picks up the shot off the stick, deflecting it into the glass.
Pressing harder now, the Hawks come tumbling over the boards,

Billy tossing out the game plan, tapping at guys out of
sequence. "Get ready." He's got that heady feel of rolling dice
with disreputable guys in the alley again. Bloodied but fierce, Pilote
jumps in off the point and joins the rush. Stapleton too. Ken Hodge
gets all of a shot that catches Terry's one good arm and spins him
around. Wharram tips a screamer into the mask.

You hear the crunch of ice and bones in front,
Horton, Stanley, Hillman and Pronovost, clearing pucks
and pounding Chicago forwards. Words like 'game' and 'players'
hardly fit what's happening here. Billy's pacing, flustered
by the mask—this is Sawchuk's fifth game in a week,
the building's an oven, a closet of smoke,

and Billy wants to see his face. Besides, you get
the heebie-jeebies when he looks at you, that yellow mask
like a corpse that's lain in no man's land a week. The fans curse
both teams, who would you want to murder, your own guys
or bloody Sawchuk? This was getting personal. And then,

as if the roof beam slowly gives beneath its load of snow,

you feel the whole building sag as Terry turns and hurls
himself onto the crossbar, fighting for a puck behind his net.
Who'd seen *that* before? Wharram looks up in alarm
at the mask coming out of the lights.
How many ways could he find to stab your heart?
The guy was making up the game as he went.

Cruising past the crease, Mikita contemplates the dangling
skates. Now Billy's talking out loud, but to himself.
Here's the guy, they said, who'd lost his fire, who'd fold the tent
when things got tough. You see him slide back to the ice
and sag against the crossbar. Billy shakes his head.
What depths had Pilote disturbed?

What creature had those words stirred up?
He glances down the bench at his marvellous beaten team,
wondering what was the one thing missing. That summer he seemed
distant, people said, his mind perhaps never far from that *one thing*
and half in dread of figuring it out. Mohns was the guy
with the last good chance to save the game,

Mohnsie, Terry's team-mate in his Boston days,
who knew his trouble there, who knew what a son of a bitch
he could be in one-on-one, and there was more than the usual ten-spot
riding on this one. In too close to let the big shot go, he swept across
the crease, turning inside out his bag of tricks, but in that close,
he had to be distracted by the arm that dangled,

the eyes that burned and followed his every move,
every waggle and dip, refusing to take the bait, the more he tried
and failed, the more he felt like a fool until there was nowhere to go,
nothing to do but lift a soft one into the pads and everybody
knew it then, they were done. Seven minutes to go and all
they could muster was two shots, both feeble.

Not with a bang but a whimper, the headline jeers,
and in the morning Billy lays the paper down

and looks out his kitchen window. What bloody dunce
comes up with lines like that to end a brilliant season on, a bad joke.
He folds the paper closed and looks out past the deepening
green in his garden. Nothing but a goddamned bad joke.

April 15, 1967
at Chicago Stadium

Toronto 4, Chicago 2

First Period

1. TOR Walton 2 (Stemkowski, Pappin) pp 6:16
2. CHI Angotti 2 (Pilote) 9:31
3. CHI B. Hull 4 (Hay, Jarrett) 11:01
4. TOR Mahovlich 3 (Keon, Walton) pp 14:14

Penalties – Horton TOR (interference) 2:36; D. Hull CHI (hooking) 5:05; Stemkowski TOR (highsticking), Van Impe CHI (highsticking) 9:09; Hodge CHI (hooking) 11:41; Hay CHI (hooking) 13:24; Pulford TOR (holding) 15:48; Pulford TOR (roughing), Nesterenko CHI (roughing) 19:28.

Second Period

No scoring.

Penalties – Stanley TOR (charging) 3:19; Wharram CHI (slashing) 5:32; Pappin TOR (holding) 7:10; Pappin TOR (highsticking) 13:12; D. Hull CHI (holding) 17:03.

Third Period

5. TOR Stemkowski 2 (Pulford, Pappin) 2:11
6. TOR Pappin 3 (Pulford, Horton) 17:14

Penalties – Stemkowski TOR (tripping) 4:23; Stemkowski TOR (tripping) 10:13; Angotti CHI (slashing) 13:54; Pulford TOR (highsticking), Mikita CHI (highsticking) 19:28.

Shots on Goal

TORONTO	7	9	15	—	31
CHICAGO	12	15	22	—	49

Goaltenders	Time	SA	GA	ENG	W/L
TOR Bower	20:00	10	2	0	—
TOR Sawchuk	40:00	37	0	0	W
CHI DeJordy	60:00	27	4	0	L

PP Conversions TOR 2/6 CHI 0/7

No Country for Old Men

(i)

I'd like to leave hockey like that. In good style.
Someone read his lips and wrote it down.

Bedlam drowned the words themselves. An uproar
after the miracle, jubilation, the clatter of sticks flung down
on the dressing room floor like crutches in a pile,
hair-stuck tape and plaster peeled away.
Down to the raw, gap-toothed, wrapped in towels,
the shouts and candour of the showers, though each
of the Leafs had stopped to speak a word or two to Terry,
each taking in the open flap of undershirt, the old man's bones
like a washboard. *Where the devil does he find it?*

The seeming fleshless legs without their pads.

(ii)

Half undressed he slumps
against the wall, no one says a word
about the cigarette in his hand. He'd drink a 7 UP
but can't get up and wouldn't ask. A fog billows out
of the showers. Bare feet flap the marshy floor.
Cautiously, the press guys squeeze between the massive flanks
and watch their backs—a snapping towel could tear your ear,
or worse, take the arse right out of your suit.
A little getting even masked as a joke.

A Leaf or two has slipped away and the older guys
are quieter now, more thoughtful, knotting ties,
one by one they sense a deepening silence in the room
and turn to look where Terry's resting, panting, having
wrestled off his sodden shirt. Their eyes tell them
armload of plums, say peacock's plumage.
Their fingers pause in their intricate task. *Jesus, Ukey,*

153

someone breaks the silence. The whole room
gapes at the hammered chest and belly. Easy to count
the darker nine or ten from Hull. They can't even look
at the shoulder, but watch as he peels off the infamous underwear
and heads without a word toward the showers.

These were guys who'd paid their dues,
who'd seen it all. But this was a moment that got their attention,
seeing what they'd asked of him that night.

(iii)

Funny how a mirror only messed you up,
or even trying to think it through.
Just let your fingers tie the tie. Good way to play
the game, itself, they would have said in those days. Gingerly,
they bent to reach their shoes, feeling bumps and bruises
of their own. Maybe what the papers said was so,
maybe it wasn't a game for old men.
But, Jesus, that just made the winning sweeter.
One to go against the Hawks, then the last great battle
of a Golden Age (they'd read). Few here had a philosophic bent,
but these were thoughtful times, the country taking its pulse
and all, a World's Fair and a waking nation's riots where
they'd meet an ancient enemy in Montreal.

The players timed it so they left the dressing room
alone. Their day might be nearly done, but they knew
things wouldn't be so bitter if they walked away a winner.
Each risked a glance behind, then closed the door.

Sometimes you really didn't like the guy.
He pissed you off, he wouldn't talk. In warm-up,
stepped away from shots he didn't want. But this was war
and all of that meant squat. You gave your goalie room.
They'd got their look at what he paid for what he did.
Besides, they knew they weren't going
anywhere without him.

Telegrams from Newfoundland

"Trouble comes in threes," he'd heard
his mother say. Her gloom would grow darker
whenever his father came home.

The first one followed a late-season game
when he'd blanked Chicago 3 to 0—*Congratulations on
reaching shutout 100.*
                    And who'd been on the other bench
but Hall—the ancient rivalry would flicker now and again
but, by then, Detroit had traded each to make room for the other,
then dumped them both. The sender seemed self-assured
and frugal—*A high-water mark none'll match.*
Terry thought he recognized the name.

The second came after he beat the Hawks in six
with Hall in goal for the final game, the last
he would play for Chicago.
                    Those zero-zero ties—how far
from that night they seemed, but they'd been fierce,
the first games after the trade, Hall and Sawchuk battling
head-to-head. Back-to-back scoreless ties. Neither gave an inch,
but over the years, you sensed a kind of truce between them.
Hall had said how much he'd learned by watching Terry
at the other end. As Terry had watched him take a shot
in the mouth a couple of nights before, the first teeth Hall
had lost, and 25 stitches to close a nasty cut. And here he was
in goal again, just as, after that blast from Watson long ago,
Terry had spit out his broken teeth and taken the stitches
without anaesthetic to keep them from recalling Hall.
Ironies tumbling over ironies. The trade to Boston
and the ties had happened the year the team had gone
to Newfoundland. *Congratulations on beating Chicago,*
the second telegram read, *the boys wish best against Montreal.*

But then the Forum brought him crashing down.

Bone-tired from battling Chicago, the bridge
of his nose cut, hammered into the crossbar, and taken out
hard by Balon, Terry let six get by him, losing game one,
then six in game four, losing again. Though Bower,
not fully recovered himself, had salvaged
the two games in between.

Terry was weak in that second defeat. He fought
the puck all night, got caught off the post, waving at pucks
that were already past him. "It wasn't the best game
I ever played," he said, "and it wasn't the worst."
The press found little comfort in a philosophical goalie.
Some said maybe he'd shot his wad in Chicago.
Some were more bitter, sneering he looked hungover.
Put simply, Backstrom was better that night. Béliveau too.
"Some days you stop 'em," says Terry,
"and some days you don't."

And no one knew better how fast the tune
could change and telegrams travel.
Here was the third in his hand and hurled to the floor
before he'd lit his first cigarette—*Congratulations in order
Terry boy,* it read, *how much did you get?*

He watched as water from the showers
darkened the words away, but he would see them
more than once that night, brooding in a lounge downtown
and later in a sleepy taxi travelling east on *rue Pie IX,*
and waking in a reassuring stranger's bed.

Game Five Again

After the off-night in Toronto—that telegram
and closing down another corner bar (*You know who that is
doncha? Over there? All by himself? A bloody sieve is what he was
tonight*)—he walks right into Montreal and stops them cold.
How often had he done that over the years.
When Toe Blake told his team that Terry'd be the one
with Bower gone, they'd found it hard to hide the grins. *Advantage
to the good guys. Tabernacle!* Now they had those clutching,
grabbing bastard sons of bitches where they wanted them.
How many shaky goalies had the Forum buried.

But this time it was Terry's turn, this time
he gets Backstrom early in the game—Ralph tries
that little move again to get an open shot, but Terry sees
what's on the way and slides across and slams the door.
Then Yvan Cournoyer's in, set up by Béliveau, then Béliveau
himself, point-blank, then Yvan again, but when he turns
to shoot, he almost drops his stick. All he sees
is Terry charging out to knock him down.

Blake knows that rebounds are his only hope
that night. He knows the signs: Sawchuk's seeming lack
of interest in the game, the lowered head like someone shot his dog,
the lazy sweeping in the crease, but lightning-quick and always
where he had to be. Toe contemplates the sagging spirits
on his bench, Tremblay talking to himself, silent Henri
punching at the air. Why they always give themselves away,
he doesn't understand. He knows the bounce it gives the other guy
and, glumly, darkly, turns away to pace and think. Who to put
out with who, the coach's alchemy, the fusion he'd found
so often in the battle's heat before.
The thought of losing to Imlach made him ill—
those craning peacock looks across the ice, that endless
taunting in the press, it made him tired. Such crude
psychology, so transparent. It made him
mad it made him mad.

The Last Faceoff

(i) *Imlach's gamble*

55 seconds on the clock and holding. Toe
smells hope. A goal behind, the game would be decided
down in Sawchuk's end, the crucial faceoff to his left—that would
take his trapper out of play. The situation shortens up the ice, Toe
pulls Worsley for the extra man. Garbage is the one hope now,
something off the blocker or the far side pad.
Terry knows what's on the way.
He knows exactly what Blake's looking for.
The mask had taken in the gathering at the bench, Toe
leaning close to give his last commands. The mask had taken in
the glance from Ferguson, the look of murder on his face.
Then watched as Blake removed his hat and smoothed
his hair, wanting every detail in its place.

Still, finesse would take a back seat now—Ferguson
would try to ram the puck and Terry through the post. Imlach,
street wise, has a counter plan. He understands the shifting
scale as well as anyone. Name the referee who'd call him
now and here, at home. Who had the balls? And stalls
to rest a tired ageing team. On the goal that closed the gap,
how bad had Duff made Horton look, Stanley too, and here was
goddamn Blake back in the game again. Imlach argues, curses, climbing
up his players' backs, "Hey faceoff in the neutral zone, hey wake up ref,
the puck went off their guy, hold it, look, for Godsake, Sawchuk's got
a problem with his gear." And when he feels they're ready, slowly,
climbs back down and out they come, Horton, Stanley, Kelly,
Armstrong, Pulford. (Three defencemen?) "Stanley takes
the faceoff ." (Stanley? What was Imlach smoking? No one
tries that bulldog tactic any more, he'll never get away with it.)
Stanley backs out. Starts to think. He hasn't taken one
in how long? Years. And he knows who's there in the circle,
calmly waiting, Béliveau, with Backstrom on the point,
and Ferguson, the talker, out in front.

His mind goes blank. He glides back in.

(ii) *underdogs*

What's this about? The crowd goes strangely quiet,
staring at the empty net. Unthinkable somehow.
Worsley. What a card. Out for a leisurely skate like that
towards their bench. Then they heard the gate crunch shut
and he was gone. They had to look again. In even the fiercest
Toronto fan, there was a grudging recognition of hockey's royalty.
Who could believe an unattended net in the Montreal end?
Who'd have thought Toe, with his dark inventiveness,
his intuition with his bench, with Béliveau, Richard and
Backstrom up the middle, a Trinity, no less, and others spoken of
with reverence in Quebec, Cournoyer, Rousseau, J. C. Tremblay,
Jacques Laperrière, the scary Ferguson, not to underestimate
the lingering heat of the Rocket, of Harvey and Lach
and Morenz—that was the nightmare, how do you grapple
with ghosts?—who'd believe that Blake would be
the one to weave the desperate plan?
The building holds its breath.

Huddled at the bench, his players ponder Toe's
tumultuous temper. They gaze at the puck-flecked boards,
listening to his plan. How the devil had they let it come to this?
Spring of 1967, something brilliant on its way, and what a thing
he fashions now in their heads, to dodge another bullet here
and get that seventh game at home against an ageing
English team, a goalie who'd owned them, past his prime—
a dream, what better way to end the age and get a leg up
on the next. And Montreal that summer with its international fair,
its brand new subway and its big league baseball team.
Then that Gallic fist of freedom in the air.

Bugger all that, said Imlach. What he dreamt about
was beating Toe. De Gaulle was just the icing on the cake.
But any thought of heading back to Montreal, of facing
Toe Blake in a seventh and deciding game at home,
had him dashing for the nearest cubicle.
He knew *this* game was the one they had to win.
They had to grab that faceoff in their end.

(Two days later, who did I see staring bleakly
into the empty Forum but the future Prime Minister
of Dominica. His mood was grim. He'd had his fill of
sleet and cold. Losing to the Leafs was hard to take.
We crossed St. Catherine Street and headed east
toward the Toe Blake Tavern where we honed our plans
to meet in paradise and talked away a nasty afternoon.
He felt something ending too, and more than school. He hadn't
met Gaddafi yet or Castro. His hero then was Béliveau. We had no
sense of what was on its way. No thought that it would fall to me
to count off troops in combat gear, the dread Van Doos,
and send them over the river into the city.
We kept a careful watch that day, but only in the hope
of seeing Worsley coming through the door.

That was the day, if things had fallen into place,
they would have played the seventh game.)

     (iii) *the Béliveau stare*

He glides back in. Then glances to see how Montreal
lines up. The ice feels cluttered, disordered, things heat up
whenever someone has the extra man. He feels the old familiar
belly-rolling fear. *You take the faceoff.* He'd felt the weight
of Imlach's hand on his shoulder. He knows what he brings
to this one is a whole career. And Béliveau, the captain,
calmly waits. *Le Gros Bill,* who'd brought a new dimension
to the game, whose size and scoring touch were such, not even
the brashest prairie boy would dare to mock his elegance and grace.
As well, he had that levelling stare, the eyes that cut you down
without a word. He wasn't beaten often when the game
was on the line—that's why they don't forget
the few defeats. Unfair of course.

Inching forward, hardly more than leaning
as the linesman sets to drop the puck, Stanley checks,
his forward motion transferred to the rising stick which jumps
and nicks the puck before it hits the ice. Somehow it lands
between his skates, he lets it go and takes a chance,

stepping into a stretching Béliveau. The puck
slides to a tantalizing stop. Sawchuk's welded to the post.
Ferguson jumps but Kelly's quicker. Fixed on running over
Kelly to the net, he lunges with an awkward check, if anything
propelling Kelly faster to the puck, who tips it neatly
through the tied-up captain's legs, where driving
Pulford picks it up. A game of speed and fortitude, for sure,
but inches too. And luck. Toe can hardly bring himself to look
as Pulford banks and, deftly off an outside edge, slides a backhand
pass, just beyond the reach of Backstrom's frantic dive,
to Armstrong flying up the ice. Coolly now, Toronto's captain
takes a look and lets it go. Five degrees his margin of error.
The puck skips into the undefended net.

What just happened here?
Had Punch and Stanley read the moment well
and stretched the rules? Had something distracted Béliveau,
putting him back on his heels a hair? Before the puck was dropped
he'd turned to take a long and searching look at Ferguson in front,
perhaps to set the plan to crash the net. Or maybe he found
it faintly distasteful, resorting to Ferguson's style
in a crisis. Perhaps in itself that seemed a kind
of defeat. Something out of the bumptious west.
Or perhaps he was only tired—he wasn't that wild
about Toronto's tactics either. The way they clipped
your wings and wore you down. Try to get loose for a pass,
you always had somebody grabbing your stick or holding your arm
in front of the net. Whatever it was, he'd lost a big one. A miracle
of timing, that's what it took—even so, he knew
that he'd been beaten to the puck.

(iv) *any sensible goalie*

"Toughest series I ever lost," says Toe. And hard
as it was, he heads out onto the ice in search of Punch,
thinking how Stanley had made him look like a genius.
Though Terry was the one who'd forced Blake's hand,
he hadn't even had to touch the puck.

Anticlimactic, perhaps, but just how any sensible goalie
would have it. Besides, he'd done his share with 47 saves.
And 55,000 minutes of life under fire—and feeling them
all in that moment—was surely more than his share
if he never touched a puck again. "Here he is,
you fucking negative Nellies, here's our Horatio,"
the happy foul-mouthed Imlach hugs his battered goalie
and brays at the press, "you know, that guy
who guards the fucking bridge."

Echoing Billy after the semifinals with Chicago,
Toe tells his guys how proud he was of how they played,
"But Sawchuk was too much tonight."

Terry takes a pounding from his own guys now
that carries him back to those heady days in Detroit.
And here's Marcel and Kelly with him still.
How strange life is. How drained they seem.
They'd borrowed what they needed, like him, from God
knows where. A fleeting thought of his wife and seven kids
comes unaccountably into his head. But here in the wild abandon
of a winning dressing room, he knows that this is where he
lives. He savours the perfect moment with a cigarette,
speaking to no one in particular, "I wonder what that
fellow thinks about it now." The telegram
had driven him back to draw on what he'd been.
What he's going on about, nobody has a clue, and none
thinks to ask. *Goalies,* they mouth to one another cheerfully.
Everybody knows they have their dark and bloody
ways of dealing with the world.

And popped the corks and let the celebrations
loose. What a feeling, oh my Jesus. Something about
surviving the heat of war, something about the plunder
yet to come. If this was the last, if this meant
the long lull was about to descend,
what a hell of a way to go.

Tidal Fears

the mind clings to the road it knows
— Mary Oliver, "Robert Schumann"

"I'm through. This is it.
You saw me out there and I was shit."

Terry, talking to some friends outside the Stadium
players' gate. A little accidental poem of embarrassment
after the opening game in Chicago.
The noisy crowd had loved it when he seemed
a moody beat-up goalie winding down.
Cheerfully they sang him off the ice.
Good bye Terry good bye,
Good bye Terry good bye,
We'll see you again but we don't know when,
Good bye Terry good bye.
How many times that season had he tried to call it
quits. His back was bad, the famous crouch had left its mark,
two ruptured vertebrae, he couldn't straighten up. He couldn't sleep
two hours at a time. You'd hardly think of it as fun, the years
of nerves before a game, the lashing out, the guilt,
the dreaded waking up and being wide awake at 3 a.m.,
of getting drilled by pucks, his nose half ripped away,
his eyeball sliced, the backs of both hands
opened up by skates.

What was it kept him going?
You'd think you'd want October with your family
in the woods, making up for awful times, or jumping on the course
behind the house, the rustle of leaves beneath your feet,
one last round before a killing frost,
or stretching out and reading by the stove.

You'd think at forty you'd feel silly
getting dressed with thirty other guys, buckling on
a flaccid garter belt and wearing regulation ties and making
wisecracks on the bus. What always brought him back

for one more year? Seven kids who needed shoes?
The skim of ice on puddles in the fall?
A tidal fear of being swept to sea?

"Hell, you saw me out there"—same guy,
ten days later, same place, after shutting down the Hawks.

("I got no squawks," said Billy Reay, a man
who saw the game in its entirety, "the guy they had
in goal was just too good.")

"Hell, you saw me out there—I can play this game forever."

VIII. LAST MINUTE OF PLAY

Think of the long trip home.
Should we have stayed at home and thought of here?

– Elizabeth Bishop, "Questions of Travel"

The Season of Wayward Thinking

The first killing frost last night.
The cat leaves tracks across the lawn,
and squash vines droop like vague summer plans.
I take a long walk, thinking of Terry after all the years,
the leaves letting go all around me in the sun.
Some plunge to the ground like fanatical pilots, some loop
and tumble, some slide back and forth, prolonging the moment
of settling. Styles of departure. I'm up to my ankles
in golden leaves, half conscious of looks
from passing cars.

Someone on the bus asked Bill White once
what was on his mind. The Hawks had come to Halifax
to play an exhibition game. The bus sat idling at a light
on South Park Street and Bill was quiet, looking out at the trees
in the Public Gardens. White was your classic stay-at-home
defenceman, your solid team guy, architect of victory.
"Burning leaves," he said, looking out at the workers who leaned
on their rakes by the fires. "The smell of burning leaves,
it always makes me think of home."

Long speech for Bill. In the moment of silence
that followed, you heard the well-tuned engine, then the clap
of laughter like a shot across the bow. "You hear what
Big Bill said?" Even the driver from Dartmouth
had to smile, though he could hear how everyone was fond
of Bill. Simple world. The lumber for the other guys,
the horse laugh for your own. The laughter echoed loudly
on the bus. The young guys up for a look were a little careful,
anxious to make a proper impression. Up in the jump seat,
Billy Reay took in the autumn scene. He looked at the golding
trees and the last of the flowers, he looked at the sloping
dreamers by the fires, and made a note to keep an eye
on Bill for a game or two. The young wolves let their eyes
slide past his place of privilege, their ears pricked up
at something in the way he spoke.

Tunnel to Windsor

(i)

So how did you feel when you let that one in
at the end? What is it with you and bouncing shots?

My mask on the floor looks blankly up at me.
I see the pens cocked, the crowd around me like a choir.
Drag your ass into the showers, I tell myself, maybe you'll drown.
"Boys. Who do you think you're talking to here?
A poet? A fucking philosopher?"

So here I am again, it seems,
a third time in the city I call home. "Insurance,"
Gadsby told a doubting press, "those intangibles a veteran
like Terry can bring to a team." Ten or twelve games at the most
is what he said to me. Surprisingly, the press has been kinder
to Crozier and me than they should, Calder Cup winners,
both of us, grinning in open relief when the other guy
or Edwards gets the call.

The crowds are snarly, though, recalling
what we used to be. And here's the city itself in ruins,
brick buildings tumbled down. Vagrants lean against
what's left of the walls. Grass and burdocks
grow up through the rubble.
Strangest of all, the gaping absence on Grande River
where once the Olympia opened its doors to the surging crowds
and horns and slamming cab doors. Someone let me go in
with a light one night before they tore it down.
The boards and glass and seats were gone.
I worked my way around to where the wives of the players
sat, trying to find their line of sight to the goals.
The building was eerily silent.
Shattered glass and plaster wherever I shone
my light, wires and cables dangling, twisting lazily.
Felt like I was walking under the sea.

I switched off the light and stood a long time listening.
Voices all around me in the dark.

Terry, how do you leave a game like that at the rink?

(ii)

I only come out of the showers after they're gone.
Sons of bitch reporters. Won't they ever leave me alone?
I take my time getting dressed and help an old attendant
gathering gear before the rats get after the salt.
Then grab a taxi to take me over to Windsor,
where Adams brought me once to look at the lights
of Detroit. You take the tunnel now, but you can see the last
of the train bridge on the Windsor side, weedy pilings pointing off
in all directions. The traffic inches toward the entrance,
sinking into a sea of blinking signal lights.

Not a happy sight for a tired goalie.

(iii)

Under the river, half the lights are out
and you think about where you are. So let the roof
come down, what do I care? *Tell us what you thought when*
Terry tell us what went through your. . . Christ, boys.
Stop the bloody puck. What the hell else
would you want on your mind?

I settle back into the worn upholstery and think
about Pat turning up at the game tonight, a rare event,
Marcel and some of the guys went over to say how glad
they were to see her. Then I think about that soft one at the end,
the let-down crowd, their cat calls and laughter climbing the stairs.
She'd be staring down into her lap, I knew, like when we were
younger, not wanting to hear, clenching her nails
so hard her palms would bleed.

At night, her hands would brush my face,
the ridges of scars touching mine. Before all the other
began. All that other, I hardly know when.

The taxi reeks of its evening fares. Perfume
and cigarettes. Anxiety and defeat.
Under the flickering lights of the tunnel I close my eyes
and shift my tired legs. At some point, it's just too late
to turn back. When I glanced up after the goal,
I couldn't find her in the leaving crowd.
And where would you go to start again? All cities
are the same, all neighbourhoods and streets.

I sense the taxi slowing down, something snarling
traffic up ahead. This tunnel's not a place you'd choose
to stop with water leaking everywhere.

Still, I'm strangely at ease with myself
tonight, knowing an old friend waits in an ancient
haunt, knowing, too, that near this river once I might have
been all I hoped to be, the guy you'd want behind you
when the game was on the line. The guy you'd leave
behind to guard the town. That cuts a bit,
but I'm safe enough down here with my thoughts.
Then I see the eyes in the mirror and a brow as dark
and scarred as my own. *So, Mr Goalie,* he murmurs
over his shoulder, *the word's out that you're leaving town
again, what does it feel like being a three time loser?*

Bachelors

(i)

A word you don't hear much anymore,
it makes us flinch like so much else. Terry's last year
with the Rangers, Orland Kurtenbach had him and Stewart over often.
"Good guys both of them," he says. He'd mention Sunday dinner
after practice, picking through the scattered gear.
As if it were them doing him a favour.

Driving home, he'd think about them sharing
someone else's summer house, shouldering past the family
photos of tennis pairs and soft-haired girls in riding hats.
Padding down the hall to shave, you'd barely see the one locked
room, the locked garage, the toppled barbecue behind the house.
He shuddered at the thought. "Did you ask the bachelors?"
That was Laurel from the kitchen. He leaned against the door
a moment in the warmth and smell of baking ham.
How strange to think of him a bachelor, with seven kids.
But that was at the heart of it somehow. Something
like anger momentarily flared, something
like a nagging sense of guilt—
what was that about?

Terry would often come early, straight off the ice,
when Orland liked to bathe his kids. He seemed
content to sit alone downstairs, the TV low. You wondered
what went through his mind, hearing the splashing and mindless
bath-time banter overhead, the soothing reassurance as the toughest
battler of his time shielded soapy water from a daughter's eyes.
Once, when they came running laughing to their mother
wrapped in towels, Terry smiled and mentioned how
he'd always loved the smell of baby powder.

That night in bed, she said she couldn't
speak, she had to turn away.

"He was mainly quiet over dinner," Orland says.

(ii)

Emile Francis used him sparingly that year,
spelling Eddie Giacomin. Eight games
was all he got into, same as in 1950 with the Wings.
Bookends for a long career. He knew Emile couldn't keep him
for another year. Terry was a legend even then, Kurtenbach recalls.
There were always stories. Driving in this morning,
he thought about the time that Toppazzini cracked his head
in Terry's crease. No one noticed he was badly hurt—the pileup
fierce, the pivotal moment in the game. Any other time,
a goalie would have whacked him with his stick, but Terry
saw the eyeballs roll and reached down with his catching glove
to cover up his face. You could see it coming after
in the dressing room—some reporter wanting
to make a story of it, and show "the surly goalie's
other side." Terry looked up dangerously,
"Wake the fuck up. Why would I take
myself out of the play like that?"

"I think he felt like he was in a trap. Seven kids to feed
and what would he do for the rest of his life? Then the talk
of a divorce again—and who could blame her?—
and his father getting badly hurt like that."

"The funeral was terrible."

Across the table, he glances at his watch
and pushes to his feet. "Gotta go," he says. He'd be
sixty anyhow, but still he towers over the table. He looks
at me a moment, thinking over all he's talked about.
"I said I had an hour—here it's almost noon.
Guys from our day, we still have to work to live."

River of Ponds

You hardly know the Rockies here in Vail. The four-lane
passing overhead. Designated parking underground. Had I only dreamt
my childhood terror in the Crowsnest Pass? "Those days are gone,"
he says. "Move on." Six hundred dollars here will get a night
in a hotel. A hundred more and you can ski
with Nesterenko for a while.

His face is ragged in the bar's expensive mirror.
Still, I know it easily, the way I recognize the rudely scalloped
planks that frame the glass—wood from stalls that horses like our own
had gnawed, bored with winter nights or worried by the howling
in the fields. "Windsuckers. Eerie sons of b's," my father
would say. "Sure as hell you'll have one or two."
At night in the frosty barn, you'd hear them grind
away at the wood, wheezing as they sucked in the frozen air.

The waiter brings me a German beer and Eric
something soft. "I was fishing on the Island once," he says.
"River of Ponds. You know the place?" They'd banked in off
the sea, and landed on some lake. Middle of nowhere. Saved his life,
he says. You never see another soul. The lazy river in the sun
is what he won't forget, the tint of amber in the pools,
and all the birds—the loons, the whistlers, so close
to the water, the single ducks or pairs, the way they'd bullet
back and forth like messengers. He sips at his juice.
"Some guys had a hard time at the end." He glances
past the doubled bottles in the glass. "Don't talk to me
about a Slavic mood—you can find a way to save yourself.
You have to want to, though. I won't say more."

He says he hopes I'm not pissed off. Tells me even here
in Vail, there's more than what you see—once you're over the back
and into the bowls. You're up in the clouds, a thousand turns
from home. You slide your tips out over the edge and pray.

"Hell, this is only where I come to warm my feet."

New York Hospital: I.C.U.

He opened one eye, half expecting Lefty's anxious face
above him in the crease. But the smell of antiseptic—what that said
to him was Spring. And it was Emile in an awkward chair asleep.
A door latched heavily down the hall. The drapes were
drawn. Looked like half the morning slipped away.

He stared at his withered arms. Nice to be not alone,
you ought to know how to say. He'd never been much like
Harvey, who quit as New York's coach when none of his players
would go for a drink with him, even Worsley politely declined.
With Indianapolis, Doug had his three young friends
from Newfoundland, ever-willing drinking companions—
good guys, but never quite good enough to get into a game. Harvey
came down to the lobby one morning, tossing out sweaters for a team
of their own. On the front he had *Harvey's Hilton Hornets,*
on the back, the number of their rooms.
That was the day the boys were driving home.

Go home yourself, Emile. Go home to your wife
and get some sleep in a proper bed. Emile, the Cat, the only
coach he'd had who'd known the life of playing goal.
That was why he kept the four-day vigil all alone.

Terry couldn't look away from his withered arms.
Where had everything gone? "Stupid, Stupid," what had
led to this. "I started it, I finished it," he snarled at his questioners,
the old blood rising at the end. Detectives like bloody reporters
with their pens. Yes, he was the one. How dextrously
a goalie hangs the chains of culpability around his neck.
Open the door to the roaring darkness,
let him go first.

Fear what was on the way?
What could there be about fear he didn't know?
Open the door.
Infinity is just another fucking number.

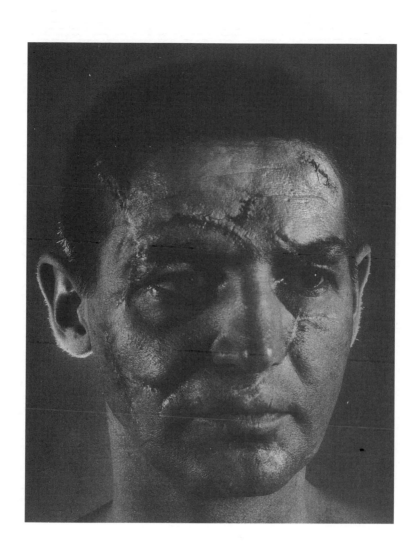

Acknowledgements

Earlier versions of some of these poems have appeared in various journals and anthologies:

"Different Ways of Telling Time," originally entitled "Kids from Edmonton," in *TickleAce* 37 (Confederation Edition), St. John's, NL, 2000; "Night Crossing in Ice," in *TickleAce* 37, reprinted in *Coastlines: The Poetry of Atlantic Canada*, eds. Anne Compton et al., Goose Lane Editions, Fredericton, N. B., 2002; "Let's Go Dancing" in *TickleAce* 37, reprinted in *The Backyards of Heaven: An Anthology of Contemporary Poetry from Ireland and Newfoundland & Labrador*, eds. John Ennis and Stephanie McKenzie, Waterford Institute of Technology, Waterford City, Ireland and Scop Productions, Corner Brook, NL, 2003; "Solid Ground" in *The Backyards of Heaven*, 2003; "Better Days," originally entitled "The Lake of No Moon Whatsoever," in *Arc* 50 (A Tribute to Don Coles at 75), Ottawa, Summer, 2003; "Desperate Moves," "One of You," and "Things in Our Day" in *The Way It Looks from Here: Contemporary Canadian Writing on Sports*, ed. Stephen Brunt, Random House, Toronto, 2004; "Sheet Metal," "The Back Door Open Where She's Gone to the Garden," "Guys like Pete Goegan," and "*Et toi, Marcel*" in *The New Quarterly* 94, Kitchener-Waterloo, Ontario, Spring 2005; "How Things Look in a Losing Streak" in *Poetry Ireland Review*, Dublin, May 2006; "Narrow Gauge" and "Game Days" in *The March Hare Anthology*, ed. Adrian Fowler, Breakwater Books, St. John's, 2007.

A word about the 'historical' nature of the book. I have used the names of actual players and coaches and referees throughout this book because of the resonance and sense of reality those names bring to the poems. And because it would be unimaginable not to do that. Also unjust. Those named here are some of those who helped to make this game such an important part of the lives of Canadians and northern Americans, particularly in the time of the great six-team league in the fifties and sixties that is the focus of this work. What appears in the poems is based on stories told to me by those listed gratefully below or on what I have read or on what I brought to the book from my own life and playing days. As far as pure veracity is concerned, I don't know which of the three would be the most unreliable. In his day, my father was known throughout the Canadian Air Force as much for his stories as for the horses he kept and moved from base to base when he was transferred. In his penultimate posting to Maritime Command in Halifax, he arrived with his family followed shortly after by forty-two horses that had travelled east by train filling two cars. As for his stories, they were less cumbersome and costly to transport and I heard the best of them many times. At some point in my life, I began to notice that each time I heard them they were a little different and mostly they seemed a little better. Since then I have come to accept the idea that factual history is simply too elusive. In my senior level university English course in non-fiction, one of the basic themes is that there is no such thing. In addition to my father, my teacher in this is Tolstoy who, in *War and Peace*, dismisses the factual historian as "a deaf man trying to answer questions that no one has asked him." So, to get at what I believe to be fiction's greater truth in writing about the life of Terry Sawchuk, the position he played in his chosen sport and the place of that sport in his age and in society generally, I have taken some liberties with the apparent facts. I have imagined Terry's thoughts and, in some cases, shuffled dates and attributed the actions or words of one person to someone altogether different. So no one else should be held accountable for what I've said that they said or thought or did between the covers of this book.

Home

John Ashton, Nick Avis, Rex Brown, Tom Daniels, Gerald Dwyer, Tony Fabijancic, Alex Faulkner, Jamie Fitzpatrick, Doug Forbes, Adrian Fowler, Gerald Goosney, Doug Grant, Pauline Hayes, Blair Kelly, Father Joe Kelly, Jim King, Walter LeMessurier, Dave MacDonald, Colin MacKenzie, Kirk McCulloch, Stephanie McKenzie, Lloyd Mercer, David Morrish, Dee Murphy, Dave Pardy, Holly Pike, Alex Powell, Christopher Pratt, Wilbur Sparkes, Dan Stewart, Austin Taylor, Steve Walsh, Paul Young.

Away

Gary Bergman, Butch Bouchard, Johnny Bower, Carl Brewer, Davorin Cikovic, Don Coles, Jim Devellano, Bill Dineen, Ken Dryden, Ron Ellis, John Ennis, Red Fisher, Emile Francis, Trent Frayne, Cal Gardner, Danny Grant, Doug Grant, Glenn Hall, Bobby Hull, Dick Irvin, Red Kelly, Orland Kurtenbach, Ted Lindsay, Laura Lush, Alistair MacLeod, Mac McDiarmid, Don McKay, Dickie Moore, Scotty Morrison, Eric Nesterenko, Marty Pavelich, Kenny Reardon, Gerry Regan, Larry Regan, Jane Rodney, Judy Sawchuk, Ron Sawchuk, Kevin Shea, Sean Smith, Karen Solie, Dan Somers, Allan Stanley, Red Storey, Bill White, Johnny Wilson, Lefty Wilson, Lorne Worsley.

Special thanks to Wade Bowers and Pam Parsons of Sir Wilfred Grenfell College, Phil Pritchard and Craig Campbell of the Hockey Hall of Fame, Stephen Brunt (sorry about the sushi), Tom Boyne, my brother, Darryl, my son, David, and daughters, Adriana and Jane (wouldn't have made it without you guys). And Anne. And Stan. You two. Nice feeling when you learn to trust someone with your life and your work. I took seven or eight years to put together *Timely Departures,* my first collection of poems. With this present book, however, I really didn't want to rush things. And I expect I might have gone on forever, talking to people about the man and the game and the age and writing the poems. It was Stan Dragland who saved me, a friend and an editor with all the skills. Thanks as well to Kitty Lewis and Alayna Munce at *Brick Books,* also Don McKay, Barry Dempster, and Maureen Harris.

I also want to acknowledge the contributions of The Hockey Hall of Fame, Sir Wilfred Grenfell College and Memorial University of Newfoundland, The Canada Council, The National Archives of Canada, the CBC, the Newfoundland Archives, the Newfoundland Hockey Hall of Fame, the Public Archives of Nova Scotia, the libraries of Memorial University, York University and Wayne State, Michigan. Also the great hockey writers of the game in its Golden Age, Red Fisher, Trent Frayne, Milt Dunnell, Scott Young; also *The Hockey News* (especially Marshall Dann and Roger Barry) for the informative articles over the years.

The Photographs

p. 177. Marc Bauman, originally published in *Look* magazine.
　　　　Terry Sawchuk.

* A poor quality print of this photograph was found in the Sawchuk files
in the archives at the Hockey Hall of Fame. No source was listed. Every
effort was made to try to find where this came from. It's likely an old
Toronto Telegram shot as it's very much like others from game six of the
1967 Toronto-Detroit series (see the photo on p. 144) which are housed
in the Clara Thomas archives of York University. However, a search of all
the negatives held in this collection failed to turn up one for this particular
shot. This negative is partly interesting because of the heavy touching up it
has been given (see Sawchuk's right hand, hair and shoulder line as well as
Haggart's right arm). Why this was done and who has done it are lost in
time.

Bibliography

Adrahtas, Tom. *Glenn Hall.* Vancouver: Greystone Books, 2003.

Berger, Howard. *Maple Leaf Moments.* Toronto: Warwick, 1994.

Bock, Hal. *Save.* Toronto: Avon, 1974.

Brooks, Kevin, and Sean Brooks, eds. *Thru the Smoky End Boards.* Vancouver: Polestar, 1996.

Butler, Hal. "Goalie With a Complex." *Sport Magazine.* February 1958: 19.

Buffey, Vern. *Black and White and Never Right: A Hockey Referee.* Mississaugua, Ontario: John Wiley & Sons, 1980.

Cole, Stephen. *The Last Hurrah: A Celebration of Hockey's Greatest Season, '66—'67.* Toronto: Penguin, 1995.

Cruise, David, and Alison Griffiths. *Net Worth: Exploding the Myths of Pro Hockey.* Toronto: Penguin, 1992.

Davis, Degan. "Hockey." *The New Quarterly,* No. 94 *(Hockey Write in Canada).* Ed. Jamie Fitzpatrick. Spring 2005: 9.

Diamond, Dan, and Eric Zweig. *Hockey's Glory Days: The 1950s and '60s.* Kansas City: Andrews McMeel, 2003.

— ed. *The Official National Hockey League 75th Anniversary Commemorative Book.* Toronto: McClelland & Stewart, 1991.

— ed. *Years of Glory: 1942-1967.* Toronto: McClelland & Stewart, 1994.

Dryden, Ken. *The Game.* 2nd ed. Toronto: MacMillan, 1993.

Dryden, Steve, ed. *The Hockey News: Century of Hockey.* Toronto: McClelland & Stewart, 2001.

Dupuis, David. *Sawchuk: The Troubles and Triumphs of the World's Greatest Goalie*. Toronto: Stoddart, 1998.

Eskenazi, Gerald. "Nassau Grand Jury Exonerates Stewart After Hearing on Sawchuk's Death." *New York Times* 9 June 1970: 1.

—. "Sawchuk of Rangers Dies Here Following 'Horseplaying' Injury." *New York Times* 1 June 1970: 1.

Fischler, Stan. *Fischler's Illustrated History of Hockey*. Toronto: Warwick, 1993.

Frayne, Trent. *Famous Hockey Players*. Toronto: Dodd Meade, 1973.

—. "Power and Production: Jack Adams's Red Wings." *The Official National Hockey League 75th Anniversary Commemorative Book*. Ed. Dan Diamond. Toronto: McClelland & Stewart, 1994.

—. "The Awful Ups and Downs of Terry Sawchuk." *MacLean's Magazine*. 19 December 1959: 50.

Haché, Alain. *The Physics of Hockey*. Baltimore: Johns Hopkins. 2002. Rpt. Vancouver: Raincoast Books, no date.

Harrison, Richard. *Hero of the Game*. Toronto: Wolsak and Wynn, 1994.

Hunt, Jim. *Men in the Nets: Hockey's Tortured Heroes*. Toronto: McGraw Hill, 1972.

Irvin, Dick. *In the Crease*. Toronto: McClelland & Stewart, 1995.

Kendall, Brian. *Shutout: The Legend of Terry Sawchuk*. Toronto: Penguin, 1996.

Kennedy, Michael P. J. *Going Top Shelf: An Anthology of Canadian Hockey Poetry*. Surrey, BC: Heritage House, 2005.

Klein, Jeff Z., and Karl-Eric Reif. *The Hockey Compendium: NHL Facts, Stats, and Stories.* Toronto: McClelland & Stewart, 2001.

Leonetti, Mike. *The Game We Knew: Hockey in the Fifties.* Vancouver: Raincoast, 1997.

McFarlane, Brian. *One Hundred Years of Hockey.* 2nd ed. Toronto: Summerhill, 1990.

Plante, Jacques. *Goaltending.* Toronto: Collier MacMillan, 1972.

Purdy, Al. *The Collected Poems of Al Purdy.* Toronto: McClelland & Stewart, 1986.

Storey, Red, with Brodie Snyder. *Red's Story.* Toronto: MacMillan, 1994.

Weir, Glenn, Jeff Chapman, and Travis Weir. *Ultimate Hockey.* Toronto: Stoddard, 1999.

R andall Maggs' poetry has appeared in
a 1994 collection, *Timely Departures*
(Breakwater Books), and in various
international reviews and anthologies, including
TickleAce, *Poetry Ireland Review*, *The Backyards
of Heaven: An Anthology of Contemporary Poetry
from Ireland and Newfoundland & Labrador* (eds.
John Ennis and Stephanie McKenzie) and *The
Way It Looks from Here: Contemporary Canadian
Writing on Sport* (ed. Stephen Brunt). With John
Ennis and Stephanie McKenzie, he is an editor of
However Blow the Winds, a collection of Irish and
Newfoundland poetry and song and *The Echoing
Years*, a collection of Irish and Canadian poetry.
As well, he has been a long-time participant in
Newfoundland's March Hare Festival of words
and music and its Artistic Director since 2002.
For the last thirty years, he has lived on the west
coast of Newfoundland and has taught Canadian
Literature and Creative Writing at Sir Wilfred
Grenfell College in Corner Brook.

Randall Maggs has played a lot of hockey himself,
though the Maggs who made it to the NHL was
his brother Darryl.